Contemporary

Foundations

Math

McGraw Hill Wright Group

The McGraw-Hill Companies

Photo Credits

Photo on cover, © Tony Weller/Digital Vision/Getty Images
Photo on page 1, © Steven Belanger/Shutterstock Images, LLC
Photo on page 75, © Getty Images.
Photo on page 98, © Kyle Smith/Shutterstock Images, LLC
Photo on page 123, © David Young-Wolff/Photo Edit
Photo on page 157, © moodboard/Corbis

www.WrightGroup.com

 **Wright Group**

Printed in the United States of America

Send all inquiries to:
Wright Group/McGraw-Hill
P.O. Box 812960
Chicago, IL 60681

ISBN: 978-1-4045-7637-7
MHID: 1-4045-7637-1

4 5 6 7 8 9 10 CCI 12 11

The **McGraw·Hill** Companies

CONTENTS

Introduction

Welcome to Contemporary's *Foundations: Math*. This book will help you build math skills so you can solve everyday problems at home, on the job, and in school.

This book is divided into five units.
>**Whole Numbers**
>**Money**
>**Decimals**
>**Fractions**
>**Ratios and Percents**

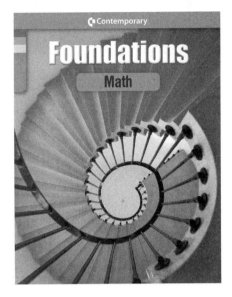

Exercises will help you review the **addition, subtraction, multiplication,** and **division** facts. You will practice **rounding numbers** and **estimating** answers. Each chapter provides opportunities to solve **word problems**.

These special features in *Foundations: Math* will help you improve your math skills.

On Your Calculator—detailed instructions that will guide you through the steps for adding, subtracting, multiplying, and dividing on your calculator

Math Note—definitions, examples, and explanations of symbols in boxes where you can easily find them

Math Talk—activities you can do with a partner or a group to help you practice using math in everyday situations

Language Tips—explanations, pronunciations, study hints, and background information that will help you understand what you are reading

Test Skills—a reminder that this skill is often tested on standardized tests

Posttest—a test, answer key, and evaluation chart that will let you know how well you have mastered the skills

We hope you will enjoy *Foundations: Math*. We wish you the best of luck with your studies!

Foundations

Contemporary's *Foundations* is a series of books designed to help you improve your skills. Each book provides skill instruction, offers interesting passages to study, and gives opportunities to practice what you are learning.

In addition to *Foundations: Math*, we invite you to explore these books.

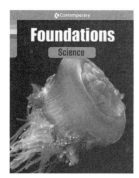

- In *Foundations: Science*, you will learn about the **human body, plant biology, physics, chemistry,** and **Earth science.**
- You will practice putting events in **order**; reading **diagrams, charts,** and **graphs**; using the **scientific method**; and making **comparisons and contrasts.**
- **Try It Yourself!** activities will guide you through simple experiments so you will have a better understanding of what you have been reading about. **Writing Workshops** and **Language Tips** will help you use your reading and writing skills to think about science topics.

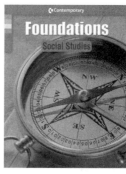

- In *Foundations: Social Studies*, you will learn about **world history, U.S. history, civics and government, geography,** and **economics.**
- You will **summarize**, make **predictions**, infer the main idea of **cartoons**, find information on **maps**, and read various kinds of **graphs**.
- **Background Information, Language Tips,** and **Writing Workshops** will let you use what you already know as you read and write about social studies topics.

- In *Foundations: Reading*, you will read **practical information, nonfiction, poetry,** and **short stories.**
- You will learn to find the **main point** and the **details**; identify **fact, opinion,** and **bias**; make **inferences**; read **photographs** and **cartoons**; and understand **rhythm, rhyme, plot,** and **theme.**
- **Writing Workshops, Language Tips,** and **prereading questions** will help you become a better reader, writer, and thinker.

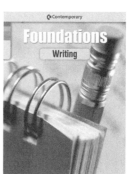

- In *Foundations: Writing*, you will practice the four steps to writing an essay: **prewriting, drafting, revising,** and **editing.**
- You will read and write five kinds of essays—**descriptive essays, personal narratives, how-to essays, essays of example,** and **comparison-and-contrast essays.**
- A language-skills workbook gives you **grammar, punctuation,** and **sentence structure** practice.
- **In Your Journal, With a Partner,** and **Language Tips** will help you become a better writer—and a better reader and thinker.

UNIT 1

Whole Numbers

In this unit, you will learn how to

- identify number places and their values

- read and write whole numbers

- round and estimate numbers

- add, subtract, multiply, and divide whole numbers

- use a calculator to solve and check problems

Chapter 1

Whole Number Basics

Count to ten.

Most likely you said, "1, 2, 3, 4, 5, 6, 7, 8, 9, 10." These are the first ten **counting numbers**. The entire set of counting numbers and **zero** (0) are called **whole numbers**. Whole numbers never end. They go on forever.

Besides using whole numbers for counting, we can use whole numbers for purposes such as these:

- to rank a group of people or things (that is, to put them in order: first, second, third, and so on)

- to measure amounts or quantities

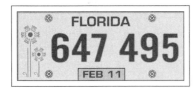

- to identify people, places, and things such as addresses and license numbers

In this chapter, we will study what makes up a whole number and how a whole number gets its **value**.

Talk Math

Do these activities with a partner or a group.

1. Make a list of items in your wallet or purse that have numbers on them. What do the numbers represent (for example, an account or an address)?
2. With a partner, take turns counting people or things in the classroom.

Whole Number Places

LANGUAGE Tip

0, 1, 2, 3, and so on, are digits. Fingers and toes are also called digits.

The number 97 has two **number places**. The number 3,684 has four number places. In each place is one of the ten symbols or **digits** that we use to write whole numbers. The ten digits in our number system are 0, 1, 2, 3, 4, 5, 6, 7, 8, and 9.

The value of a digit depends on its place in a number. The diagram below shows the names of the first four whole number places. The diagram also shows an example of a four-digit number with each digit written below its place name. Notice the comma between the digits 3 and 6. A comma is often used to separate the thousands place from the hundreds place.

> The digit 3 is in the thousands place. It represents 3 thousands, or 3,000.
> The digit 6 is in the hundreds place. It represents 6 hundreds, or 600.
> The digit 8 is in the tens place. It represents 8 tens, or 80.
> The digit 4 is in the ones place. It represents 4 ones, or 4.

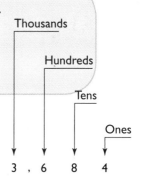

Exercise 1

1. In the number 784, which digit is in the ones place? _____

2. In the number 784, which digit is in the hundreds place? _____

3. What is the value of the digit 8 in 784? _____

4. What is the value of the digit 1 in the number 2,196? _____

5. Which digit in 2,196 is in the ones place? _____

6. What is the value of the digit 2 in 2,196? _____

7. In the number 2,196, what is the value of the digit 9? _____

8. Which of the following has the *largest* digit in the hundreds place?

    a. 8,693   b. 728   c. 2,927   d. 1,213

9. Which of the following has the *smallest* digit in the thousands place?

    a. 4,185   b. 2,766   c. 3,821   d. 6,744

10. Which of the following has the *largest* digit in the tens place?

    a. 3,916   b. 335   c. 5,147   d. 184

Check your answers on page 185.

Place Value and Zeros

Think about these three numbers.

        3,009   3,090   3,900

        Each number has four number places.

        Each number is written with just three digits: 0, 3, and 9.

The digit 0 has no value, but it plays an important role in our number system. Zero is a **placeholder**.

Exercise 2

1. In 3,009, zeros hold the _____ place and the _____ place.

2. In 3,090, zeros hold the _____ place and the _____ place.

3. In 3,900, zeros hold the _____ place and the _____ place.

4. What is the value of the 9 in the number 3,900? _____

5. What is the value of the 3 in the number 3,090? _____

6. What is the value of the 9 in 3,090? _____

Check your answers on page 185.

The diagram below lists the names of the first seven places in our whole number system. It also shows an example of a seven-digit number with each digit written below its place name. A comma separates the millions place from the hundred thousands place. Another comma separates the thousands place from the hundreds place. The number 6,073,500 has three zeros. Zero works as a placeholder in the hundred thousands place, in the tens place, and in the ones place.

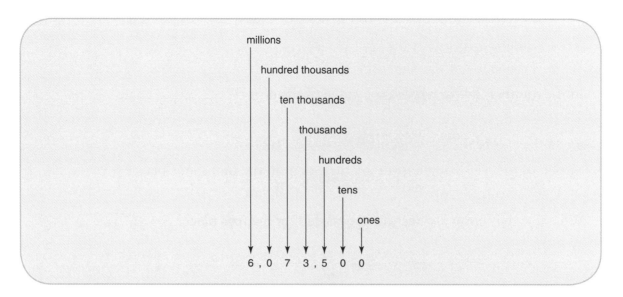

Exercise 3

Fill in the blanks to complete each statement.

1. In the number 307, zero holds the _____ place.

2. In 730, zero holds the _____ place.

3. In 1,056, zero holds the _____ place.

4. In 2,040, zeros hold the _____ place and the _____ place.

5. In 5,008, zeros hold the _____ place and the _____ place.

6. In 20,650, zeros hold the _____ place and the _____ place.

Use the number 134,600 to answer questions 7–10.

7. What digit is in the thousands place? _____

8. The digit 3 is in what whole number place? _____

9. What is the value of the digit 4? _____

10. What is the value of the digit 1? _____

Use the number 2,978,000 to answer questions 11–14.

11. What is the value of the digit 8? _____

12. The digit 2 is in what whole number place? _____

13. What digit is in the hundred thousands place? _____

14. What is the value of the digit 7? _____

Check your answers on page 185.

Reading and Writing Whole Numbers

To read and write whole numbers, pay close attention to zeros and commas. Zeros work as place holders. Commas separate the place names into groups of three.

Commas are in the same position in numbers written with digits as they are in numbers written with words.

> **Math Note**
>
> The = sign is called an **equals** sign. It means that one value is equal to, or the same as, another value.

Read each example carefully.

> 8,300 = eight thousand, three hundred
> 27,060 = twenty-seven thousand, sixty
> 904,520 = nine hundred four thousand, five hundred twenty
> 6,130,200 = six million, one hundred thirty thousand, two hundred

Exercise 4

Fill in the blanks to write the number with words.

1. 31,600   = thirty-one _____, six _____

2. 5,012   = five _____, twelve

3. 93,500   = ninety-three _____, five _____

4. 210,000   = two hundred ten _____

5. 186,400   = one hundred eighty-six _____, four _____

6. 2,850,000 = two _____, eight hundred fifty _____

7. 9,007,050 = nine _____, seven _____, fifty

8. 4,062,100 = four _____, sixty-two _____, one _____

Use digits to write each of the following numbers.

9. three hundred five = _____

10. four hundred twenty = _____

11. nine hundred twelve = _____

12. two thousand, one hundred = _____

13. three thousand, four hundred six = _____

14. eight thousand, fifteen = _____

15. fifteen thousand, one hundred fifty = _____

16. one hundred seventy thousand = _____

17. three hundred four thousand, nine hundred twelve = _____

18. five million, three hundred thousand = _____

19. seven million, ten thousand, four hundred twenty-five = _____

Write each number in words.

20. 436 = _____

21. 508 = _____

22. 1,740 = _____

23. 6,014 = _____

24. 12,300 = _____

25. 35,210 = _____

26. 65,300 = _____

27. 100,054 = _____

28. 420,000 = _____

29. 8,600,000 = _____

30. 3,419,000 = _____

Check your answers on page 185.

Rounded Numbers

We often use **rounded numbers** instead of exact numbers when we talk about amounts. A rounded number is an approximate value rather than an exact value. Usually rounded numbers end in one or more zeros. For example, you might say you are driving "about 60 miles per hour" when your exact speed is 64 miles per hour.

Rounded numbers are easy and quick to work with. People like to use tens (10, 20, 30, etc.), hundreds (100, 200, 300, etc.), and thousands (1000, 2000, 3000, etc.).

To round a number to a specific place, look at the digit to its right. If the digit to the right is less than 5, round down. If the digit to the right is 5 or greater, round up.

Use the ≈ sign when you round numbers. It means "about" or "approximately equal to."

Round 87 to the nearest ten.
In 87, the digit 8 is in the tens place.
Since the digit to the right is 7, round up. 87 ≈ 90

Round 213 to the nearest ten.
In 213, the digit 1 is in the tens place.
Since the digit to the right is 3, round down. 213 ≈ 210

Round 4,056 to the nearest hundred.
In 4,056, the digit 0 is in the hundreds place.
Since the digit to the right is 5, round up. 4,056 ≈ 4,100

Round 7,489 to the nearest thousand.
In 7,489, the digit 7 is in the thousands place.
Since the digit to the right is 4, round down. 7,489 ≈ 7,000

Math Note

The = sign means *equals*.

The ≈ sign means *is about* or *approximately equal to*.

Exercise 5

Round each number to the nearest ten.

1. 28   ≈ _____
2. 31   ≈ _____
3. 65   ≈ _____
4. 121   ≈ _____
5. 158   ≈ _____

6. 526   ≈ _____
7. 811   ≈ _____
8. 2,307 ≈ _____
9. 3,255 ≈ _____
10. 10,426 ≈ _____

Round each number to the nearest hundred.

11. 218   ≈ _____
12. 180   ≈ _____
13. 452   ≈ _____
14. 2,349 ≈ _____
15. 4,822 ≈ _____

16. 5,077 ≈ _____
17. 10,147 ≈ _____
18. 22,836 ≈ _____
19. 88,615 ≈ _____
20. 131,464 ≈ _____

Round each number to the nearest thousand.

21. 2,448 ≈ _____
22. 3,276 ≈ _____
23. 4,083 ≈ _____
24. 7,561 ≈ _____
25. 11,206 ≈ _____

26. 13,651 ≈ _____
27. 56,560 ≈ _____
28. 102,386 ≈ _____
29. 422,647 ≈ _____
30. 687,509 ≈ _____

Check your answers on page 185.

The Calculator

Throughout this book, you can use a calculator to find and check answers. This diagram shows the basic parts that you should find on all calculators. Read about each part and then find that part on your calculator.

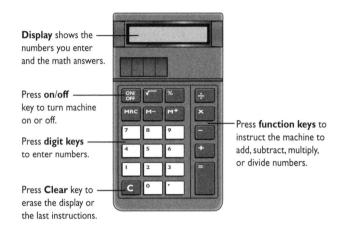

Display shows the numbers you enter and the math answers.

Press **on/off** key to turn machine on or off.

Press **digit keys** to enter numbers.

Press **Clear** key to erase the display or the last instructions.

Press **function keys** to instruct the machine to add, subtract, multiply, or divide numbers.

Before you enter a number for a new problem, press the **C** key. This clears the display. It is like starting with a clean, blank page.

Exercise 6

Answer these questions about your calculator.

1. Turn your calculator on. What do you see in the display?

_____

2. Press the **3** key until the display is full of threes. How many digits does the display show?

_____

3. Press the **6** key. Then press the **C** key. What does the display show?

_____

Check your answers on page 185.

Entering Numbers

To enter a number on your calculator, press the keys in the same order that you read the digits. Enter each digit, always moving from left to right, until the number shows on your display. If you make a mistake, press the [C] key and start again.

> Enter 190
> Press the digit keys [1] [9] [0]   Read the display [190.]

In this example, the display shows a decimal point after the ones place. Some calculators do not show decimal points after whole numbers. Does yours?

Exercise 7

Practice entering these numbers into a calculator. Press the [C] key after you enter each number.

1. 3	4. 98	7. 1,490	10. 47,090
2. 8	5. 201	8. 3,837	11. 842,688
3. 40	6. 568	9. 12,656	12. 2,696,000

Points to Remember

- Each digit in a whole number gets its value from its place.

- Zeros are placeholders that keep other digits in their places.

- Use commas to separate the thousands place from the hundreds place and the millions place from the hundred thousands place.

- The symbol = means *equal to*.

- The symbol ≈ means *about* or *approximately equal to*.

- To round a number to a specific place, look at the digit to its right. Round up if the digit to the right is 5 or greater. Round down if the digit to the right is less than 5.

Whole Number Basics Checkup

1. In the number 437, which digit is in the tens place? _____

2. What is the value of the 8 in 1,852? _____

3. Which digit is in the thousands place in 813,405? _____

4. What is the value of the 6 in 56,209? _____

5. Fill in the blanks to express the number 7,314 in words.

   seven _____, three _____ fourteen

6. Fill in the blanks to write 260,908 in words.

   two hundred sixty _____, nine _____ eight

7. Write the number one thousand, two hundred thirty with digits. _____

8. Write twenty-eight thousand, seven hundred fifty with digits. _____

9. Write seven hundred thirty thousand, one hundred forty with digits. _____

10. Write 860 in words. _____

11. Write 9,503 in words. _____

12. Write 14,090 in words. _____

13. Round 627 to the nearest ten. _____

14. Round 841 to the nearest hundred. _____

15. Round 43,096 to the nearest thousand. _____

16. Round 508,700 to the nearest ten thousand. _____

17. On these calculator keys, write the order that you would enter the number "three hundred fifty-eight."

Check your answers on page 185.

Chapter 2

Test Skill

Addition and Subtraction Facts

In Chapters 3 and 4, we will study addition and subtraction. First, we will review the basic facts that addition and subtraction are built on.

Addition is the operation of combining numbers. When you add, you get a **sum** or a **total**.

LANGUAGE Tip

The word *operation* means "work." The question *What operation would you do to solve this problem?* means "What kind of work (addition, subtraction, multiplication, or division) would you do?"

You have **2 stamps**, and you buy **3 stamps**. You now have **5 stamps**.

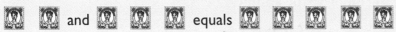

When a number is added to 0 (zero), the total is the number you added to 0. You have **0 stamps**. You buy **3 stamps**. You now have **3 stamps**.

0 and 🖼️ 🖼️ 🖼️ equals 🖼️ 🖼️ 🖼️

Numbers can be added in any order; the total will be the same.
2 stamps and **3 stamps** are **5 stamps**.
3 stamps and **2 stamps** are **5 stamps**.

🖼️ 🖼️ and 🖼️ 🖼️ 🖼️ equals 🖼️ 🖼️ 🖼️ 🖼️ 🖼️

🖼️ 🖼️ 🖼️ and 🖼️ 🖼️ equals 🖼️ 🖼️ 🖼️ 🖼️ 🖼️

Exercises 1–4 will help you review the addition facts. The problems are organized in columns by their sum.

Math Note

The basic facts are written with the equals sign (=). The amount on one side of the sign is equal to the amount on the other side.

$$2 + 3 = 5 \qquad 0 + 3 = 3 \qquad 3 + 2 = 5$$

Basic Addition Facts

$$6 + 4 = 10 \leftarrow \text{sum}$$
$$\uparrow$$
$$\text{the plus sign means to add}$$

Addition facts can be read in several ways:
Six and four equals ten.
Six added to four is ten.
Six plus four equals ten.

Exercise 1

Fill in the missing numbers to complete the addition facts.

Sum of 1	Sum of 2	Sum of 3	Sum of 4
1. $0 + \rule{1cm}{0.4pt} = 1$	3. $0 + \rule{1cm}{0.4pt} = 2$	5. $0 + \rule{1cm}{0.4pt} = 3$	8. $0 + \rule{1cm}{0.4pt} = 4$
2. $1 + \rule{1cm}{0.4pt} = 1$	$1 + 1 = 2$	$1 + 2 = 3$	$1 + 3 = 4$
	4. $2 + \rule{1cm}{0.4pt} = 2$	6. $2 + \rule{1cm}{0.4pt} = 3$	$2 + 2 = 4$
		7. $3 + \rule{1cm}{0.4pt} = 3$	9. $3 + \rule{1cm}{0.4pt} = 4$
			10. $4 + \rule{1cm}{0.4pt} = 4$

Check your answers on page 185.

Exercise 2

Study each column of addition facts. Fill in the missing numbers.

Sum of 5	Sum of 6	Sum of 7	Sum of 8
1. $0 + \rule{1cm}{0.4pt} = 5$	5. $0 + \rule{1cm}{0.4pt} = 6$	9. $0 + \rule{1cm}{0.4pt} = 7$	14. $0 + \rule{1cm}{0.4pt} = 8$
$1 + 4 = 5$	$1 + 5 = 6$	$1 + 6 = 7$	$1 + 7 = 8$
$2 + 3 = 5$	$2 + 4 = 6$	$2 + 5 = 7$	$2 + 6 = 8$
2. $3 + \rule{1cm}{0.4pt} = 5$	$3 + 3 = 6$	$3 + 4 = 7$	$3 + 5 = 8$
3. $4 + \rule{1cm}{0.4pt} = 5$	6. $4 + \rule{1cm}{0.4pt} = 6$	10. $4 + \rule{1cm}{0.4pt} = 7$	$4 + 4 = 8$
4. $5 + \rule{1cm}{0.4pt} = 5$	7. $5 + \rule{1cm}{0.4pt} = 6$	11. $5 + \rule{1cm}{0.4pt} = 7$	15. $5 + \rule{1cm}{0.4pt} = 8$
	8. $6 + \rule{1cm}{0.4pt} = 6$	12. $6 + \rule{1cm}{0.4pt} = 7$	16. $6 + \rule{1cm}{0.4pt} = 8$
		13. $7 + \rule{1cm}{0.4pt} = 7$	17. $7 + \rule{1cm}{0.4pt} = 8$
			18. $8 + \rule{1cm}{0.4pt} = 8$

Check your answers on page 185.

Exercise 3

Fill in the missing number to complete each addition fact.

Sum of 9

1. $0 + \underline{} = 9$
   $1 + 8 \quad = 9$
   $2 + 7 \quad = 9$
   $3 + 6 \quad = 9$
   $4 + 5 \quad = 9$
2. $5 + \underline{} = 9$
3. $6 + \underline{} = 9$
4. $7 + \underline{} = 9$
5. $8 + \underline{} = 9$
6. $9 + \underline{} = 9$

Sum of 10

$1 + 9 \quad = 10$
$2 + 8 \quad = 10$
$3 + 7 \quad = 10$
$4 + 6 \quad = 10$
$5 + 5 \quad = 10$
7. $6 + \underline{} = 10$
8. $7 + \underline{} = 10$
9. $8 + \underline{} = 10$
10. $9 + \underline{} = 10$

Sum of 11

$2 + 9 \quad = 11$
$3 + 8 \quad = 11$
$4 + 7 \quad = 11$
$5 + 6 \quad = 11$
11. $6 + \underline{} = 11$
12. $7 + \underline{} = 11$
13. $8 + \underline{} = 11$
14. $9 + \underline{} = 11$

Sum of 12

$3 + 9 \quad = 12$
$4 + 8 \quad = 12$
$5 + 7 \quad = 12$
$6 + 6 \quad = 12$
15. $7 + \underline{} = 12$
16. $8 + \underline{} = 12$
17. $9 + \underline{} = 12$

Sum of 13

$4 + 9 \quad = 13$
$5 + 8 \quad = 13$
$6 + 7 \quad = 13$
18. $7 + \underline{} = 13$
19. $8 + \underline{} = 13$
20. $9 + \underline{} = 13$

Sum of 14

$5 + 9 \quad = 14$
$6 + 8 \quad = 14$
$7 + 7 \quad = 14$
21. $8 + \underline{} = 14$
22. $9 + \underline{} = 14$

Check your answers on page 186.

Exercise 4

Study each column of addition facts. Fill in the missing numbers.

Sum of 15

$6 + 9 \quad = 15$
$7 + 8 \quad = 15$
1. $8 + \underline{} = 15$
2. $9 + \underline{} = 15$

Sum of 16

$7 + 9 \quad = 16$
$8 + 8 \quad = 16$
3. $9 + \underline{} = 16$

Sum of 17

$8 + 9 \quad = 17$
4. $9 + \underline{} = 17$

Sum of 18

$9 + 9 = 18$

Check your answers on page 186.

Basic Subtraction Facts

Subtraction is an operation that compares two amounts. When you subtract, you find the **difference** between two amounts.

You use **4** of your **5 stamps**. You have **1 stamp** left.

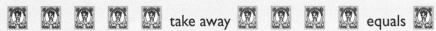

When you subtract 0, the difference is the number you started with.
You have **5 stamps**. You use **0 stamps**. You still have **5 stamps** left.

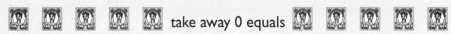

When a number is subtracted from the same number, the difference is 0.
You use **5** of your **5 stamps**. You have **0 stamps** left.

Subtraction is the opposite of addition. For every addition fact, there are two subtraction facts. From $6 + 4 = 10$, you get these subtraction facts:

$$10 - 6 = 4 \qquad\qquad 10 - 4 = 6$$

$$10 - 6 = 4 \leftarrow \text{difference}$$
$$\uparrow$$
the minus sign means to subtract

You can read subtraction facts in several ways:

Ten take away six is four.
Six subtracted from ten equals four.
Ten minus six equals four.

Exercises 5 and 6 will help you review the basic subtraction facts. The problems are organized in columns by their difference.

Points to Remember

• Addition and subtraction are opposite math operations.

• The answer to an addition problem is a *sum*.

• The answer to a subtraction problem is a *difference*.

• Numbers can be added in any order; the sum will be the same.

Exercise 5

Study each column of subtraction facts. Fill in the missing numbers.

Difference of 1	Difference of 2	Difference of 3	Difference of 4
1. $10 - \underline{\hphantom{0}} = 1$	11. $11 - \underline{\hphantom{0}} = 2$	21. $12 - \underline{\hphantom{0}} = 3$	31. $13 - \underline{\hphantom{0}} = 4$
2. $9 - \underline{\hphantom{0}} = 1$	12. $10 - \underline{\hphantom{0}} = 2$	22. $11 - \underline{\hphantom{0}} = 3$	32. $12 - \underline{\hphantom{0}} = 4$
3. $8 - \underline{\hphantom{0}} = 1$	13. $9 - \underline{\hphantom{0}} = 2$	23. $10 - \underline{\hphantom{0}} = 3$	33. $11 - \underline{\hphantom{0}} = 4$
4. $7 - \underline{\hphantom{0}} = 1$	14. $8 - \underline{\hphantom{0}} = 2$	24. $9 - \underline{\hphantom{0}} = 3$	34. $10 - \underline{\hphantom{0}} = 4$
5. $6 - \underline{\hphantom{0}} = 1$	15. $7 - \underline{\hphantom{0}} = 2$	25. $8 - \underline{\hphantom{0}} = 3$	35. $9 - \underline{\hphantom{0}} = 4$
6. $5 - \underline{\hphantom{0}} = 1$	16. $6 - \underline{\hphantom{0}} = 2$	26. $7 - \underline{\hphantom{0}} = 3$	36. $8 - \underline{\hphantom{0}} = 4$
7. $4 - \underline{\hphantom{0}} = 1$	17. $5 - \underline{\hphantom{0}} = 2$	27. $6 - \underline{\hphantom{0}} = 3$	37. $7 - \underline{\hphantom{0}} = 4$
8. $3 - \underline{\hphantom{0}} = 1$	18. $4 - \underline{\hphantom{0}} = 2$	28. $5 - \underline{\hphantom{0}} = 3$	38. $6 - \underline{\hphantom{0}} = 4$
9. $2 - \underline{\hphantom{0}} = 1$	19. $3 - \underline{\hphantom{0}} = 2$	29. $4 - \underline{\hphantom{0}} = 3$	39. $5 - \underline{\hphantom{0}} = 4$
10. $1 - \underline{\hphantom{0}} = 1$	20. $2 - \underline{\hphantom{0}} = 2$	30. $3 - \underline{\hphantom{0}} = 3$	40. $4 - \underline{\hphantom{0}} = 4$

Check your answers on page 186.

Exercise 6

Study the basic subtraction facts. Fill in the missing numbers.

Difference of 5	Difference of 6	Difference of 7	Difference of 8
1. $14 - \underline{\hphantom{0}} = 5$	11. $15 - \underline{\hphantom{0}} = 6$	21. $16 - \underline{\hphantom{0}} = 7$	31. $17 - \underline{\hphantom{0}} = 8$
2. $13 - \underline{\hphantom{0}} = 5$	12. $14 - \underline{\hphantom{0}} = 6$	22. $15 - \underline{\hphantom{0}} = 7$	32. $16 - \underline{\hphantom{0}} = 8$
3. $12 - \underline{\hphantom{0}} = 5$	13. $13 - \underline{\hphantom{0}} = 6$	23. $14 - \underline{\hphantom{0}} = 7$	33. $15 - \underline{\hphantom{0}} = 8$
4. $11 - \underline{\hphantom{0}} = 5$	14. $12 - \underline{\hphantom{0}} = 6$	24. $13 - \underline{\hphantom{0}} = 7$	34. $14 - \underline{\hphantom{0}} = 8$
5. $10 - \underline{\hphantom{0}} = 5$	15. $11 - \underline{\hphantom{0}} = 6$	25. $12 - \underline{\hphantom{0}} = 7$	35. $13 - \underline{\hphantom{0}} = 8$
6. $9 - \underline{\hphantom{0}} = 5$	16. $10 - \underline{\hphantom{0}} = 6$	26. $11 - \underline{\hphantom{0}} = 7$	36. $12 - \underline{\hphantom{0}} = 8$
7. $8 - \underline{\hphantom{0}} = 5$	17. $9 - \underline{\hphantom{0}} = 6$	27. $10 - \underline{\hphantom{0}} = 7$	37. $11 - \underline{\hphantom{0}} = 8$
8. $7 - \underline{\hphantom{0}} = 5$	18. $8 - \underline{\hphantom{0}} = 6$	28. $9 - \underline{\hphantom{0}} = 7$	38. $10 - \underline{\hphantom{0}} = 8$
9. $6 - \underline{\hphantom{0}} = 5$	19. $7 - \underline{\hphantom{0}} = 6$	29. $8 - \underline{\hphantom{0}} = 7$	39. $9 - \underline{\hphantom{0}} = 8$
10. $5 - \underline{\hphantom{0}} = 5$	20. $6 - \underline{\hphantom{0}} = 6$	30. $7 - \underline{\hphantom{0}} = 7$	40. $8 - \underline{\hphantom{0}} = 8$

Difference of 9

41. $18 - \underline{\hphantom{0}} = 9$	44. $15 - \underline{\hphantom{0}} = 9$	47. $12 - \underline{\hphantom{0}} = 9$	50. $9 - \underline{\hphantom{0}} = 9$
42. $17 - \underline{\hphantom{0}} = 9$	45. $14 - \underline{\hphantom{0}} = 9$	48. $11 - \underline{\hphantom{0}} = 9$	
43. $16 - \underline{\hphantom{0}} = 9$	46. $13 - \underline{\hphantom{0}} = 9$	49. $10 - \underline{\hphantom{0}} = 9$	

Check your answers on page 186.

Addition and Subtraction Facts Checkup

Find each sum.

1. $3 + 2 =$ ___   9. $9 + 9 =$ ___   17. $8 + 6 =$ ___

2. $6 + 1 =$ ___   10. $8 + 7 =$ ___   18. $7 + 3 =$ ___

3. $0 + 3 =$ ___   11. $6 + 9 =$ ___   19. $8 + 0 =$ ___

4. $4 + 4 =$ ___   12. $7 + 7 =$ ___   20. $9 + 6 =$ ___

5. $9 + 1 =$ ___   13. $4 + 5 =$ ___   21. $7 + 9 =$ ___

6. $6 + 7 =$ ___   14. $3 + 7 =$ ___   22. $7 + 2 =$ ___

7. $4 + 8 =$ ___   15. $6 + 6 =$ ___   23. $8 + 9 =$ ___

8. $5 + 6 =$ ___   16. $7 + 5 =$ ___   24. $6 + 5 =$ ___

Find each difference.

25. $6 - 1 =$ ___   33. $17 - 9 =$ ___   41. $15 - 6 =$ ___

26. $5 - 2 =$ ___   34. $13 - 4 =$ ___   42. $11 - 7 =$ ___

27. $8 - 2 =$ ___   35. $15 - 7 =$ ___   43. $14 - 8 =$ ___

28. $4 - 3 =$ ___   36. $16 - 9 =$ ___   44. $7 - 3 =$ ___

29. $10 - 5 =$ ___   37. $8 - 5 =$ ___   45. $18 - 9 =$ ___

30. $11 - 7 =$ ___   38. $11 - 8 =$ ___   46. $11 - 5 =$ ___

31. $13 - 9 =$ ___   39. $12 - 7 =$ ___   47. $7 - 0 =$ ___

32. $12 - 3 =$ ___   40. $13 - 5 =$ ___   48. $11 - 3 =$ ___

Check your answers on page 186.

Math Note

The addition facts and the subtraction facts are important tools that you will need as you continue to study mathematics. Take the time now to memorize any of the facts that you cannot answer quickly.

Addition

Suppose you are making a guest list for a party. You need 9 invitations. Later you add more names to your list, so you need 7 more invitations. How many invitations do you need altogether?

You need to find the total number of invitations. By combining the two numbers, you can find the answer. Count the total number of invitations shown in the diagram below.

+ 9 invitations combined with 7 invitations

The total is **16**. You need 16 invitations altogether.

Instead of counting, you can find the total by using **addition**.

> Fill in the blanks, using numbers from the diagram above.
> _____ + _____ = 16 ← **total** or **sum**
>
> numbers you need to combine

You should have filled in **9** and **7**. These numbers are called the **addends**. They are the numbers that are being added.

Things being added together must be *alike*. You can add 9 invitations and 7 invitations. But you cannot add 9 invitations and 6 dessert plates because these things are not alike.

In this chapter, you will learn the basic skills needed for adding numbers. You will practice using a calculator to get correct answers. You will also learn about estimating.

Talk Math

Do these activities with a partner or a group.

1. Talk about numbers of objects that you can combine. Be sure the items are alike.

2. Describe everyday situations where you need to add numbers to get a total.

Writing Addition Problems

Problem: A pair of children's jeans costs **$12**. A child's jacket costs **$36**. If you buy both items, what is the total cost?

To get the answer, add the numbers 12 and 36. The total cost is **$48**.

To solve an addition problem, first write the numbers you are adding in columns. Line up the numbers with ones under ones, tens under tens, and so on. Then write a plus sign (+) to show that you have an addition problem. Under the last number, draw a line. Write the sum below that line. The digits in the answer must line up with the other digits in the problem. For 12 + 36, you may write the 12 or the 36 first.

```
        tens ones              tens ones
         ↓ ↓                    ↓ ↓
          1 2         OR         3 6
        + 3 6                  + 1 2
sum →     4 8                    4 8   ← sum
```

When the numbers in an addition problem do not have the same number of digits, be sure the ones are under the ones and the tens are under the tens.

Rewrite the problem 25 + 671 with the correct digits under each other.

```
        tens ones              tens ones
         ↓ ↓                    ↓ ↓
          2 5         OR         6 7 1
        + 6 7 1                + 2 5
sum →     6 9 6                  6 9 6   ← sum
```

Exercise 1

Set up an addition problem for each pair of numbers. Do not solve the problems.

1. 35, 18   3. 161, 465   5. 255, 99   7. 96, 3   9. 153, 68

2. 44, 20   4. 230, 304   6. 437, 8   8. 49, 207   10. 75, 411

Check your answers on page 186.

Solving Addition Problems

To solve an addition problem, write the numbers with ones under ones, tens under tens, and so on. Add the digits, beginning with the ones column. Finally, write the sum under each column.

LANGUAGE Tip

Antonyms

Vertical means "up and down."

Horizontal means "from side to side."

Add 36 + 12.
Write the problem with ones under ones and tens under tens.

      3 6   First add the ones: 6 + 2 = 8.
    + 1 2   Then add the tens: 3 + 1 = 4.
      4 8   The sum is 48.

Exercise 2

Write each problem with the numbers aligned vertically. Then solve each problem.

1. 12 + 17 =   **2.** 312 + 155 =   **3.** 14 + 33 =   **4.** 161 + 224 =

Check your answers on page 186.

When the numbers in an addition problem do not have the same number of digits, be sure the ones are under ones and the tens are under tens.

Add 347 + 51.
Write the problem with ones under ones and tens under tens.

      3 4 7   Add the ones: 7 + 1 = 8.
    +   5 1   Add the tens: 4 + 5 = 9.
      3 9 8   Add the hundreds: 3 + nothing = 3.
                   The sum is 398.

Exercise 3

Write each problem with the digits aligned in columns. Then solve each problem.

1. 523 + 34 =   **2.** 45 + 923 =   **3.** 1,716 + 82 =   **4.** 57 + 2,341 =

Check your answers on page 186.

Adding Zeros

When the numbers in an addition problem include zeros, add the zeros to the other digits in their columns.

> Add 40 + 28.
> Write the problem with ones under ones and tens under tens.
>
>   4 0   Add the ones: 0 + 8 = 8.
> + 2 8   Add the tens: 4 + 2 = 6.
>   6 8   The sum is 68.

Exercise 4

Write each problem with ones under ones and tens under tens. Solve each problem.

1. 32 + 10 =   3. 40 + 30 =   5. 380 + 513 =   7. 506 + 243 =

2. 20 + 25 =   4. 204 + 192 =   6. 700 + 199 =   8. 192 + 706 =

Check your answers on page 186.

 On Your Calculator

Follow these steps to practice solving an addition problem on your calculator.

Add 12 + 36.

1. Clear your calculator.
2. Enter an addend.
3. Press the plus sign.
4. Enter the other addend.
5. Press the equals sign.
6. Read the display.

C | 1 | 2 | + | 3 | 6 | = | 48.

Carrying to the Tens Place

When you are finding a sum, only one digit can go at the bottom of each column. If the sum of the digits in a column is 10 or more, write the ones digit in the ones column. Then **carry** the tens digit to the top of the tens column. When you carry a digit, the next column to the left will have one more digit to add.

Find the sum of 25 and 17.
Write the problem with ones under ones and tens under tens.

```
    1
   2 5      Add the ones: 5 + 7 = 12.
 + 1 7        Write 2 under the ones column and carry 1 to the tens.
   4 2      Add the tens: 1 + 2 + 1 = 4.
            The sum is 42.
```

Find the sum of 408 and 265.
Write the problem with ones under ones, tens under tens, and so on.

```
    1
   4 0 8    Add the ones: 8 + 5 = 13.
 + 2 6 5      Write 3 under the ones column and carry 1 to the tens.
   6 7 3    Add the tens: 1 + 0 + 6 = 7.
            Add the hundreds: 4 + 2 = 6.
            The sum is 673.
```

Exercise 5

Add each problem. Check your answers. Redo any problems that were incorrect.

1. 15 + 27 =   4. 55 + 29 =   7. 438 + 58 =

2. 18 + 12 =   5. 48 + 47 =   8. 274 + 109 =

3. 36 + 26 =   6. 106 + 115 =   9. 56 + 217 =

Check your answers on page 186.

Carrying to the Hundreds Place

In an addition problem, when the sum of the digits in the tens column is 10 or more, you must carry to the hundreds column.

> Find the sum of 567 and 82.
> Write the problem with ones under ones and tens under tens.
>
> ```
>    1
>   5 6 7    Add the ones: 7 + 2 = 9.
> +   8 2    Add the tens:  6 + 8 = 14.
>   6 4 9       Write the 4 under the tens column and carry 1 to the hundreds.
>            Add the hundreds: 1 + 5 = 6.
>            The sum is 649.
> ```

In the next problem, you must carry to the tens column and to the hundreds column.

> Find the sum of 138 and 294.
> Write the problem with ones under ones, tens under tens, and so on.
>
> ```
>   1 1         Add the ones: 8 + 4 = 12.
>   1 3 8          Write the 2 under the ones column and carry 1 to the tens.
> + 2 9 4       Add the tens: 1 + 3 + 9 = 13.
>   4 3 2          Write the 3 under the tens column and carry 1 to the hundreds.
>               Add the hundreds: 1 + 1 + 2 = 4.
>               The sum is 432.
> ```

Exercise 6

Add each problem. Check your answers. Redo any problems that were incorrect.

1. $36 + 91 =$

2. $742 + 66 =$

3. $265 + 76 =$

4. $673 + 173 =$

5. $45 + 98 =$

6. $80 + 60 =$

7. $95 + 219 =$

8. $394 + 195 =$

9. $82 + 648 =$

10. $272 + 68 =$

11. $508 + 97 =$

12. $94 + 309 =$

Check your answers on page 186.

Adding More than Two Numbers

Add three or more numbers the same way you added two numbers. Remember that when you carry a digit, the next column will have an extra digit to add.

Marla spent $25 for a desk lamp, $39 for groceries, and $12 for dry cleaning. What total amount did she spend?

```
  I
  2 5      Add the ones: 5 + 9 + 2 = 16.
  3 9        Write 6 under the ones column and carry I to the tens.
+ I 2      Add the tens: I + 2 + 3 + I = 7.
  7 6      The sum is 76.  Marla spent $76.
```

Exercise 7

Add each problem. Check your answers. Redo any problems that were incorrect.

1. 13 + 54 + 42   =   4. 21 + 826 + 25 =   7. 11 + 24 + 33 + 42   =

2. 36 + 121 + 14 =   5. 64 + 525 + 106 =   8. 62 + 120 + 75 + 403   =

3. 123 + 15 + 432 =   6. 36 + 716 + 402 =   9. 167 + 209 + 536 + 140 =

Check your answers on page 186.

 On Your Calculator

Find the sum: 25 + 39 + 12 = _____

1. Clear your calculator.

2. Enter one addend.

3. Press the plus sign.

4. Enter the next addend.

5. Press the plus sign.

6. Enter the last addend.

7. Press the equals sign.

8. Read the display.

```
C    2 5  +  3 9  +  I 2  =    76.
```

Estimated Sums

Estimates are approximate answers. We use them when exact answers are not necessary. We also use them to see if answers are reasonable. One way to estimate when adding is to round the **lead digit** of each addend. The lead digit is the digit in the column farthest to the left. (Reread pages 8 and 9 if you need to review rounding.)

Find the exact answer and an estimate for this problem:

$$19 + 72 + 188 = ?$$

```
                1 1
                1 9      ≈          2 0     Round 19 up to 20.
                7 2      ≈          7 0     Round 72 down to 70.
              + 1 8 8    ≈        + 2 0 0   Round 188 up to 200.
exact answer → 2 7 9     ≈          2 9 0   ← estimate
```

The estimate, 290, shows that the exact answer, 279, is reasonable.

Exercise 8

For each problem, find the exact answer. Then estimate to see that each answer is reasonable. Round the lead digits, and find the sum of the rounded numbers.

1. $8 + 27 + 14 =$

2. $3 + 24 + 87 =$

3. $92 + 125 + 108 =$

4. $52 + 7 + 37 =$

5. $49 + 54 + 423 =$

6. $275 + 344 + 257 =$

7. $189 + 377 + 212 =$

8. $307 + 78 + 924 =$

9. $45 + 567 + 381 =$

10. $12 + 44 + 26 + 22 =$

11. $45 + 21 + 26 + 41 =$

12. $107 + 78 + 15 + 142 =$

Practice entering the problems in this exercise on a calculator.

Check your answers on pages 186–187.

Real-Life Addition Problems

In some real-life problems, it is not possible to get an exact answer. For example, if you are ordering pizza for five people, it is not possible to know exactly how much pizza each person will eat. In this case, you need only an **estimate**.

Exercise 9

First estimate an answer by rounding the lead digits. Then find the exact answer.

1. Five years ago, there were 8,258 people living in Johnsonville. By the end of last year, there were 826 more people. Find the population of Johnsonville at the end of last year.

Estimate	Exact

2. The driving distance from Atlanta to Savannah is 258 miles. The driving distance from Savannah to Jacksonville is 133 miles. What is the driving distance from Atlanta to Jacksonville by way of Savannah?

Estimate	Exact

3. This year Maria pays $695 a month for rent. Next year she will have to pay $41 more. Find her monthly rent for next year.

Estimate	Exact

4. An auditorium has 1,876 seats on the main floor and 468 seats in the balcony. Find the total number of seats in the auditorium.

Estimate	Exact

Read the description. Write *Estimate* or *Exact* to tell how you would solve the problem.

_____ 5. the number of gallons of paint needed to paint your bedroom

_____ 6. the number of cakes to serve at a party

_____ 7. the total bill for a customer who shopped in your shoe store

_____ 8. the amount of gasoline needed to fill your car's gas tank

_____ 9. the balance in your checkbook before deciding to buy a jacket

Check your answers on page 187.

Addition Checkup

1. $43 + 26 =$ 2. $170 + 819 =$ 3. $856 + 402 =$ 4. $38 + 1,250 + 83 + 481 =$

Find the exact answers. Then estimate to see that each answer is reasonable.

5. $296 + 71 + 380 =$ 6. $108 + 592 + 378 =$ 7. $494 + 1,208 + 736 =$

8. Franco drove 219 miles on Monday morning before he took a break. That afternoon he drove another 287 miles. How many miles did he travel altogether? Find the exact answer. Then estimate to check your work.

Exact	Estimate

9. In January the Davis family spent $428 for food, $117 on utilities, and $639 for rent. Find the total of these expenses. Find the exact answer. Then estimate to check your work.

Exact	Estimate

10. You want to know the time you need to get from your job to the restaurant where you eat lunch. Do you need an estimate or an exact answer? _____

Check your answers on page 187.

Points to Remember

- To add whole numbers, line up the numbers with ones under ones, tens under tens, and so on.

- When you add whole numbers, first add digits in the ones column.

- When the sum of a column is 10 or more, put the right digit of the sum in the column you added and carry the left digit to the next column to the left.

- One way to estimate an addition problem is to round each number to the lead digit (the digit at the left). Then add the rounded numbers.

Subtraction

LOAN PAYMENTS		
1	6	11
2	7	12
3	8	13
4	9	14
5	10	15

You bought a new sofa, and you have agreed to make 15 payments. This is your 7th payment. How many more payments do you have to make? The answer you need is the **difference** between two amounts.

This chart represents your payments. Count the number of remaining payments.

By counting, you see that you have 8 more payments to make. However, instead of counting the number of payments, you can use subtraction to find the answer. This is the problem that you need to solve. Fill in the missing numbers.

_____ – _____ = 8 ← remaining number of payments
↑   ↑
total number of payments   number of payments you have made

You should have filled in **15** and **7**.

You can also use subtraction for these purposes:

• comparing two amounts

Your sister Juanita lives **11 miles** away, and your sister Ria lives **4 miles** away. How much farther do you have to travel to visit Juanita than to visit Ria?
$11 - 4 = 7$ ← Juanita lives 7 miles farther away than Ria.

• finding how much more is needed to reach a given amount

A company offers 3 weeks of vacation after **10 years** of service. Jake has worked at the company for **4 years**. How many more years does he need to work at the company to receive 3 weeks of vacation?
$10 - 4 = 6$ ← how many more years Jake needs to work at the company

Solving Subtraction Problems

Read the following problem.

> A store sells twin-size comforters for **$99**. During its spring sale, the store lowered the price to **$75**. By how much was the price lowered?

To get the answer, subtract $75 from $99. The difference is **$24**.

Write the numbers in a subtraction problem with ones under ones, and so on. The numbers in a subtraction problem *always* follow a certain order. The top number is the amount to subtract from, and the bottom number is the amount being subtracted.

To solve a subtraction problem, subtract the digits in each column, moving from right to left. Write the difference directly below the digits you are subtracting.

> Subtract 75 from 99.
> Put the larger number, 99, on top.
>
> $$\begin{array}{r} 9\,9 \\ -\,7\,5 \\ \hline 2\,4 \end{array}$$
>
> First subtract the ones: $9 - 5 = 4$.
> Then subtract the tens: $9 - 7 = 2$.
> The difference is 24.

Exercise 1

Rewrite each problem so the number you are subtracting from is on top. Then solve each problem. Check your answers. If any answer is not correct, redo the problem.

1. $18 - 11 =$ 5. $249 - 126 =$ 9. $780 - 230 \quad =$

2. $36 - 12 =$ 6. $375 - 255 =$ 10. $928 - 904 \quad =$

3. $76 - 44 =$ 7. $49 - 25 \quad =$ 11. $609 - 403 \quad =$

4. $85 - 25 =$ 8. $483 - 162 =$ 12. $1{,}576 - 1{,}214 =$

Check your answers on page 187.

Talk Math

Do these activities with a partner or a group.

1. Describe situations in which you have to subtract to get an answer.
2. Use time (for example, minutes or hours) to show subtraction facts.

When the two numbers in a subtraction problem do not have the same number of digits, be careful when you line up the numbers. Ones should be under ones, and so on.

> Find the difference between 36 and 548.
>
> Put the larger number, 548, on top.
>
> $$\begin{array}{r} 548 \\ -36 \\ \hline 512 \end{array}$$ First subtract the ones: $8 - 6 = 2$.
> Then subtract the tens: $4 - 3 = 1$.
> Subtract the hundreds: $5 -$ nothing $= 5$. The difference is 512.

Exercise 2

1. Subtract 28 from 439. **3.** 81 subtracted from 395 = **5.** Subtract 25 from 1,056.

2. 349 minus 42 = **4.** Take 71 from 694. **6.** 6 subtracted from 759 =

Check your answers on page 187.

On Your Calculator

Follow these steps to practice solving a subtraction problem on your calculator.
Subtract 99 – 75.

1. Clear your calculator.
2. Enter the larger number.
3. Press the minus sign.
4. Enter the number to be subtracted.
5. Press the equals sign.
6. Read the display.

$$\boxed{C}\ \boxed{9}\ \boxed{9}\ \boxed{-}\ \boxed{7}\ \boxed{5}\ \boxed{=}\ \boxed{24.}$$

Practice entering the problems in Exercises 1 and 2 on your calculator.

Chapter 4

Borrowing

Sometimes a digit is larger than the digit it must be subtracted from. To subtract, you need to **borrow** 1 from the column to the left.

Subtract 62 – 13.

In this problem, the digit 3 in the ones column cannot be subtracted from 2.

5 12	Borrow 1 ten from 6. Now there are 5 tens in the tens column.
6 2	Add the 1 ten to the 2 in the ones column: $10 + 2 = 12$.
– 1 3	Subtract the new ones: $12 - 3 = 9$.
4 9	Subtract the new tens: $5 - 1 = 4$.
	The difference is 49.

Math Note

- To check a subtraction problem, add the difference to the bottom number of the problem.
- The result should equal the top number. For the last example, $49 + 13 = 62$.

Exercise 3

Solve the problems. Check your answers on a calculator. If any answer is not correct, redo the problem.

1. $24 - 16 =$ **4.** $56 - 27 =$ **7.** $81 - 17 =$ **10.** $38 - 9 =$

2. $35 - 19 =$ **5.** $72 - 25 =$ **8.** $95 - 48 =$ **11.** $52 - 7 =$

3. $48 - 39 =$ **6.** $64 - 55 =$ **9.** $25 - 6 =$ **12.** $86 - 8 =$

Check your answers on page 187.

Subtracting Larger Numbers

Now look at an example of borrowing with larger numbers.

Subtract 638 − 152.

In this problem, you can subtract the digits in the ones column, but the digit 5 in the tens column cannot be subtracted from 3.

```
  5 13
  6 3 8         Subtract the ones: 8 − 2 = 6.
− 1 5 2         Borrow 1 hundred from 6. Now there are 5 hundreds.
  4 8 6         Add the 1 hundred to the 3 in the tens column:
```

      Subtract the ones: 8 − 2 = 6.
      Borrow 1 hundred from 6. Now there are 5 hundreds.
      Add the 1 hundred to the 3 in the tens column:
        1 hundred + 3 tens = 130 or 13 tens.
      Subtract the new tens: 13 − 5 = 8.
      Subtract the new hundreds: 5 − 1 = 4.
      The difference is 486.

You may have to borrow more than once. Read the next example carefully.

Subtract 726 − 268.

```
  6 11
    1 16
  7 2 6         Borrow 1 ten from 2. Now there is 1 ten.
− 2 6 8         Add the 1 ten to the 6 in the ones column: 1 ten + 6 = 16.
  4 5 8         Subtract the new ones: 16 − 8 = 8.
```

      Borrow 1 ten from 2. Now there is 1 ten.
      Add the 1 ten to the 6 in the ones column: 1 ten + 6 = 16.
      Subtract the new ones: 16 − 8 = 8.
      Borrow 1 hundred from 7. Now there are 6 hundreds.
      Add the 1 hundred to the 1 in the tens column:
        1 hundred + 1 ten = 110 or 11 tens.
      Subtract the new tens: 11 − 6 = 5.
      Subtract the new hundreds: 6 − 2 = 4.
      The difference is 458.

Exercise 4

Solve the problems. Check your answers on a calculator. Redo incorrect problems.

1. 248 − 190 =   3. 352 − 169 =   5. 623 − 584 =   7. 734 − 99 =

2. 215 − 152 =   4. 344 − 128 =   6. 455 − 278 =   8. 284 − 76 =

Check your answers on page 187.

Borrowing with Zeros

When a zero fills the column you are trying to subtract from, borrow 1 from the next column to the left.

LANGUAGE Tip

There are two ways to spell the plural form of *zero*:

    zeros

    zeroes

The more common way is *zeros*.

Subtract 50 − 26.

```
  4 10
  5̸ 0̸
− 1 3
  3 7
```

Borrow 1 ten from 5. Now there are 4 tens in the tens column.
Add the 1 ten to the 0 in the ones column:
    10 + 0 = 10.
Subtract the new ones: 10 − 3 = 7.
Subtract the new tens: 4 − 1 = 3.
The difference is 37.

In some subtraction problems, you have to borrow two places to the left.

Subtract 506 − 378.

In this problem, you cannot subtract 8 from 6 in the ones column, and you cannot borrow from 0 in the tens column. You must first borrow from the hundreds.

```
    9
  4 1̸0 16
  5̸ 0̸ 6̸
− 3 7 8
  1 2 8
```

First borrow 1 hundred from 5. Now there are 4 hundreds.
Add the 1 hundred to the 0 in the tens column:
    1 hundred + 0 tens = 100 or 10 tens.
Next borrow 1 ten from the 10 tens. Now there are 9 tens.
Add the 1 ten to the 6 in the ones column: 10 + 6 = 16.
Subtract the new ones: 16 − 8 = 8.
Subtract the new tens: 9 − 7 = 2.
Subtract the new hundreds: 4 − 3 = 1.
The difference is 128.

Exercise 5

Solve each problem. Check your answers on a calculator. Redo incorrect problems.

1. 30 − 9 =   3. 208 − 168 =   5. 903 − 755 =   7. 900 − 248 =

2. 50 − 24 =   4. 409 − 172 =   6. 600 − 123 =   8. 800 − 570 =

Check your answers on page 187.

Estimated Differences

An estimate gives you an idea of whether an answer makes sense. You can find estimated differences by first rounding the lead digit for each number. Then subtract the rounded digits to find an estimate.

Find the exact answer and an estimate for $87 - 9$.

$$
\begin{array}{r}
\overset{7\ 17}{\cancel{8}\cancel{7}} \\
-\quad 9 \\
\hline
78
\end{array}
\qquad
\begin{array}{r}
\approx\quad 90 \\
\approx\quad -10 \\
\hline
80
\end{array}
$$

exact answer → 78   80 ← estimate

Round 87 up to 90.
Round 9 up to 10.

The estimate **80** shows that the answer **78** is reasonable.

Exercise 6

For each problem, find the exact answer. Then estimate each answer by rounding the lead digits and subtracting the rounded numbers.

1. $83 - 21 \ =$

2. $53 - 8 \ \ =$

3. $56 - 49 \ =$

4. $92 - 48 \ =$

5. $275 - 15 =$

6. $869 - 412 =$

7. $412 - 31 \ =$

8. $283 - 175 =$

9. $783 - 167 =$

10. $509 - 210 =$

11. $782 - 253 =$

12. $860 - 653 =$

13. $807 - 59 \ =$

14. $604 - 258 =$

15. $702 - 196 =$

Check your answers on page 187.

A Strategy for Solving Word Problems

We all solve math problems in our everyday lives. A strategy, or plan, can make solving problems easier. Here is one strategy that can help you.

> Fred is driving his van from his home in South Bend to Evansville, which is **303 miles** away. He stopped for gas after driving **115 miles**. How much farther does he have to drive to get to Evansville?

1. *State the problem in your own words.*

Ask yourself, "What am I looking for?" Drawing a picture may help you.

For this problem you might ask yourself, "How many more miles does Fred have to drive?" or "What is the distance from the gas station to Evansville?"

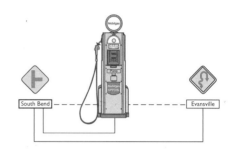

2. *List the facts.*

Ask yourself, "What numbers do I need?" For this problem, you have only two numbers—the distance from South Bend to Evansville and the distance from South Bend to the gas station where Fred stopped.

3. *Choose the mathematical operation you need.*

The phrase "how much farther" suggests a comparison. To solve this problem, you need to subtract the shorter distance from the total distance.

4. *Estimate the answer.*

Round the total distance from South Bend to Evansville to 300 miles. Round the distance from South Bend to the gas station to 100 miles.

Subtract the rounded numbers: 300 − 100 = 200 miles

Your answer should be *close to* 200 miles.

5. *Solve for the exact answer.*

Subtract 115 from 303.

Fred has to drive **188 more miles** to get to Evansville. The estimate, 200 miles, tells you that your answer is reasonable.

$$\begin{array}{r} 9 \\ 2\ \ \cancel{10}\ \ 13 \\ \cancel{3}\ \ \cancel{0}\ \ \cancel{3} \\ -\ \ 1\ \ 1\ \ 5 \\ \hline 1\ \ 8\ \ 8\ \text{ miles} \end{array}$$

To solve the problem on a calculator, press the following keys.

$$\boxed{3}\ \boxed{0}\ \boxed{3}\ \boxed{-}\ \boxed{1}\ \boxed{1}\ \boxed{5}\ \boxed{=}\ \boxed{188.}$$

Exercise 7

First estimate the answer by rounding the lead digits. Then find the exact answer.

1. The speed limit on the freeway is 55 miles per hour. In the city, the speed limit is 30 miles per hour. How much slower is the speed limit in the city?

Estimate	Exact

2. Anna drove 62 miles from Angel Falls to Elton. Then she drove 25 miles to Jackson. How many miles did she drive altogether?

Estimate	Exact

3. Sam bought items for $63 at a hardware store. He paid with $80. How much change did he receive?

Estimate	Exact

4. Alice has a work benefit of 28 vacation days each year. If she decides to take 19 days in August, how many vacation days remain for the rest of the year?

Estimate	Exact

5. Yuja wants to buy a new laptop that is listed for $490. During a Labor Day sale, the laptop is marked for $75 less than the list price. How much is the laptop during the sale?

Estimate	Exact

6. Silvia is trying to consume no more than 2,400 calories per day. On Monday her breakfast had 565 calories, and her lunch had 915 calories. If she sticks to her plan, how many calories can she eat for dinner?

Estimate	Exact

Check your answers on page 188.

Points to Remember

- The number you are subtracting from must come first.

- To subtract whole numbers, start with the digits in the ones column.

- You can borrow 1 from the next column to the left.

Subtraction Checkup

Solve each problem.

1. 78 − 33 =

3. 960 − 450 =

5. 280 − 45 =

2. 456 − 32 =

4. 233 − 106 =

6. 706 − 529 =

Find the exact answers. Then estimate each answer by rounding the lead digits and subtracting the rounded numbers.

7. 583 − 498 =

8. 692 − 357 =

9. 904 − 286 =

Solve each problem.

10. Matt is asking $950 for his used motorcycle. Steve will buy it for $825, at most. How much less than Matt's asking price is Steve willing to pay?

11. Elena makes $488 a week at her job. Her supervisor is going to raise her salary $45 a week. What will be her new weekly salary?

12. Karl weighed 214 pounds. Then he went on a diet and lost 47 pounds. How much did he weigh at the end of his diet?

Check your answers on page 188.

Multiplication and Division Facts

In Chapters 6 and 7, we will study multiplication and division. First, we will review the basic math facts that multiplication and division are based on.

Multiplication is the operation of adding a number to itself a number of times.

> You need **2 stamps** on each of **3 letters**. You need **6 stamps** in all.
>
> 3 equal groups of 🖼 🖼 equals 🖼 🖼 🖼 🖼 🖼 🖼

Remember these facts about multiplication:

- When a number is multiplied by 1, the answer is the number you started with.

  For example, $6 \times 1 = 6$.

- When a number is multiplied by 0 (zero), the answer is 0.

  For example, $6 \times 0 = 0$.

- Numbers can be multiplied in any order; the answer will be the same.

  For example, $2 \times 3 = 6$ and $3 \times 2 = 6$.

Division is the operation of separating a total into equal groups. Think of division as the operation of finding how many times one number is contained in another number.

Remember these facts about division:

- When a number is divided by the same number, the answer is 1.

  For example, $3 \div 3 = 1$.

- When a number is divided by 1, the answer is the number you started with.

  For example, $3 \div 1 = 3$.

- When 0 is divided by a number, the answer is 0.

  For example, $0 \div 3 = 0$.

- A number **cannot** be divided by 0.

In the rest of this chapter, we will review basic multiplication and division facts.

Basic Multiplication Facts

The most common symbol used to indicate multiplication is the × sign. The first number in a multiplication problem is often called the **multiplier**. The answer to a multiplication problem is called the **product**.

In the following examples, think of multiplication as a kind of repeated addition.

> What is the product of 2 × 4?
> 2 groups each containing 4 items is the same as 4 + 4 = 8.
> The product of 2 × 4 = 8.

> What is the product of 4 × 2?
> 4 groups each containing 2 items is the same as 2 + 2 + 2 + 2 = 8.
> The product of 4 × 2 = 8.

You can read multiplication facts in two ways:
  Two multiplied by four is eight.
  Four times two equals eight.

Exercises 1 and 2 will help you review the basic multiplication facts. The problems are organized in columns by the multiplier. Make sure you know the basic multiplication facts before continuing your work.

Exercise 1

Study each column. Fill in the missing products.

Multiplier: 1	Multiplier: 2	Multiplier: 3	Multiplier: 4
1. 1 × 1 = ___	10. 2 × 1 = ___	19. 3 × 1 = ___	28. 4 × 1 = ___
2. 1 × 2 = ___	11. 2 × 2 = ___	20. 3 × 2 = ___	29. 4 × 2 = ___
3. 1 × 3 = ___	12. 2 × 3 = ___	21. 3 × 3 = ___	30. 4 × 3 = ___
4. 1 × 4 = ___	13. 2 × 4 = ___	22. 3 × 4 = ___	31. 4 × 4 = ___
5. 1 × 5 = ___	14. 2 × 5 = ___	23. 3 × 5 = ___	32. 4 × 5 = ___
6. 1 × 6 = ___	15. 2 × 6 = ___	24. 3 × 6 = ___	33. 4 × 6 = ___
7. 1 × 7 = ___	16. 2 × 7 = ___	25. 3 × 7 = ___	34. 4 × 7 = ___
8. 1 × 8 = ___	17. 2 × 8 = ___	26. 3 × 8 = ___	35. 4 × 8 = ___
9. 1 × 9 = ___	18. 2 × 9 = ___	27. 3 × 9 = ___	36. 4 × 9 = ___

Check your answers on page 188.

Multiplication Facts Table

This table shows the basic multiplication facts. The numbers being multiplied are in the first column at the left and along the top row. The **products** are the numbers in the white section of the table.

To use the table, find one number you want to multiply in the column at the left. Then find the other number in the top row. The product is found where the row and the column meet.

For example, to solve 4×5, find 4 in the left column and 5 in the top row. The row and the column meet at 20. The product is **20**.

×	1	2	3	4	5	6	7	8	9	10
1	1	2	3	4	5	6	7	8	9	10
2	2	4	6	8	10	12	14	16	18	20
3	3	6	9	12	15	18	21	24	27	30
4	4	8	12	16	20	24	28	32	36	40
5	5	10	15	20	25	30	35	40	45	50
6	6	12	18	24	30	36	42	48	54	60
7	7	14	21	28	35	42	49	56	63	70
8	8	16	24	32	40	48	56	64	72	80
9	9	18	27	36	45	54	63	72	81	90
10	10	20	30	40	50	60	70	80	90	100

Exercise 2

Fill in the missing products.

Multiplier: 5

1. $5 \times 1 = $ _____
2. $5 \times 2 = $ _____
3. $5 \times 3 = $ _____
4. $5 \times 4 = $ _____
$5 \times 5 = 25$
$5 \times 6 = 30$
$5 \times 7 = 35$
$5 \times 8 = 40$
$5 \times 9 = 45$

Multiplier: 6

5. $6 \times 1 = $ _____
6. $6 \times 2 = $ _____
7. $6 \times 3 = $ _____
8. $6 \times 4 = $ _____
9. $6 \times 5 = $ _____
$6 \times 6 = 36$
$6 \times 7 = 42$
$6 \times 8 = 48$
$6 \times 9 = 54$

Multiplier: 7

10. $7 \times 1 = $ _____
11. $7 \times 2 = $ _____
12. $7 \times 3 = $ _____
13. $7 \times 4 = $ _____
14. $7 \times 5 = $ _____
15. $7 \times 6 = $ _____
$7 \times 7 = 49$
$7 \times 8 = 56$
$7 \times 9 = 63$

Multiplier: 8

16. $8 \times 1 = $ _____
17. $8 \times 2 = $ _____
18. $8 \times 3 = $ _____
19. $8 \times 4 = $ _____
20. $8 \times 5 = $ _____
21. $8 \times 6 = $ _____
22. $8 \times 7 = $ _____
$8 \times 8 = 64$
$8 \times 9 = 72$

Multiplier: 9

23. $9 \times 1 = $ _____
24. $9 \times 2 = $ _____
25. $9 \times 3 = $ _____
26. $9 \times 4 = $ _____
27. $9 \times 5 = $ _____
28. $9 \times 6 = $ _____
29. $9 \times 7 = $ _____
30. $9 \times 8 = $ _____
$9 \times 9 = 81$

Check your answers on page 188.

Math Note

Take the time now to memorize the multiplication and division facts. They are important tools.

Division Facts

One symbol that indicates division is the ÷ sign. In a problem written with the ÷ sign, the first number is the **dividend**. The dividend is the number that is being divided up. The second number is called the **divisor**. The divisor tells how many times to separate, or divide, the dividend. The answer to a division problem is called the **quotient**.

The diagram below shows the parts of a division problem.

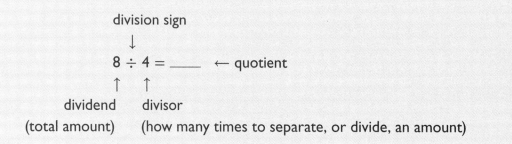

What is the quotient of 8 ÷ 4?

8 items can be separated into 2 groups each containing 4 items.
8 ÷ 4 = 2

What is the quotient of 8 ÷ 2?
8 items can be separated into 4 groups each containing 2 items.
8 ÷ 2 = 4

Division facts can be read two ways. The last example can be read like this:
    Two divided into eight is four.
    Eight divided by two equals four.
Division is the opposite operation of multiplication. The quotient multiplied by the divisor equals the dividend. For the last example, 4 × 2 = 8.

Exercises 3 and 4 will help you review the basic division facts. The problems are organized by their **divisor**.

Talk Math

Do these activities with a partner or a group.
1. Think of times when you use multiplication and division outside the classroom.
2. Create multiplication and division word problems using objects in the room.

Exercise 3

Fill in the missing quotients.

Think: What number times the divisor equals the dividend?

LANGUAGE *Tip*

Suffix

The suffix *-ion* means "the act of."

Multiplication is the act of multiplying.

Division is the act of dividing.

Divisor: 1	Divisor: 2	Divisor: 3	Divisor: 4
1. $9 \div 1 =$ ___	10. $18 \div 2 =$ ___	19. $27 \div 3 =$ ___	28. $36 \div 4 =$ ___
2. $8 \div 1 =$ ___	11. $16 \div 2 =$ ___	20. $24 \div 3 =$ ___	29. $32 \div 4 =$ ___
3. $7 \div 1 =$ ___	12. $14 \div 2 =$ ___	21. $21 \div 3 =$ ___	30. $28 \div 4 =$ ___
4. $6 \div 1 =$ ___	13. $12 \div 2 =$ ___	22. $18 \div 3 =$ ___	31. $24 \div 4 =$ ___
5. $5 \div 1 =$ ___	14. $10 \div 2 =$ ___	23. $15 \div 3 =$ ___	32. $20 \div 4 =$ ___
6. $4 \div 1 =$ ___	15. $8 \div 2 =$ ___	24. $12 \div 3 =$ ___	33. $16 \div 4 =$ ___
7. $3 \div 1 =$ ___	16. $6 \div 2 =$ ___	25. $9 \div 3 =$ ___	34. $12 \div 4 =$ ___
8. $2 \div 1 =$ ___	17. $4 \div 2 =$ ___	26. $6 \div 3 =$ ___	35. $8 \div 4 =$ ___
9. $1 \div 1 =$ ___	18. $2 \div 2 =$ ___	27. $3 \div 3 =$ ___	36. $4 \div 4 =$ ___

Check your answers on page 188.

Exercise 4

Fill in the missing quotients.

Divisor: 5	Divisor: 6	Divisor: 7	Divisor: 8	Divisor: 9
1. $45 \div 5 =$ ___	10. $54 \div 6 =$ ___	19. $63 \div 7 =$ ___	28. $72 \div 8 =$ ___	37. $81 \div 9 =$ ___
2. $40 \div 5 =$ ___	11. $48 \div 6 =$ ___	20. $56 \div 7 =$ ___	29. $64 \div 8 =$ ___	38. $72 \div 9 =$ ___
3. $35 \div 5 =$ ___	12. $42 \div 6 =$ ___	21. $49 \div 7 =$ ___	30. $56 \div 8 =$ ___	39. $63 \div 9 =$ ___
4. $30 \div 5 =$ ___	13. $36 \div 6 =$ ___	22. $42 \div 7 =$ ___	31. $48 \div 8 =$ ___	40. $54 \div 9 =$ ___
5. $25 \div 5 =$ ___	14. $30 \div 6 =$ ___	23. $35 \div 7 =$ ___	32. $40 \div 8 =$ ___	41. $45 \div 9 =$ ___
6. $20 \div 5 =$ ___	15. $24 \div 6 =$ ___	24. $28 \div 7 =$ ___	33. $32 \div 8 =$ ___	42. $36 \div 9 =$ ___
7. $15 \div 5 =$ ___	16. $18 \div 6 =$ ___	25. $21 \div 7 =$ ___	34. $24 \div 8 =$ ___	43. $27 \div 9 =$ ___
8. $10 \div 5 =$ ___	17. $12 \div 6 =$ ___	26. $14 \div 7 =$ ___	35. $16 \div 8 =$ ___	44. $18 \div 9 =$ ___
9. $5 \div 5 =$ ___	18. $6 \div 6 =$ ___	27. $7 \div 7 =$ ___	36. $8 \div 8 =$ ___	45. $9 \div 9 =$ ___

Check your answers on page 188.

Multiplication and Division Facts Checkup

Find each product.

1. $3 \times 3 =$ ___
2. $1 \times 5 =$ ___
3. $9 \times 2 =$ ___
4. $6 \times 3 =$ ___
5. $9 \times 3 =$ ___
6. $5 \times 8 =$ ___

7. $9 \times 7 =$ ___
8. $9 \times 9 =$ ___
9. $8 \times 7 =$ ___
10. $5 \times 2 =$ ___
11. $8 \times 4 =$ ___
12. $4 \times 6 =$ ___

13. $7 \times 5 =$ ___
14. $4 \times 9 =$ ___
15. $5 \times 6 =$ ___
16. $7 \times 9 =$ ___
17. $8 \times 8 =$ ___
18. $9 \times 6 =$ ___

19. $4 \times 7 =$ ___
20. $5 \times 5 =$ ___
21. $6 \times 8 =$ ___
22. $3 \times 7 =$ ___
23. $7 \times 7 =$ ___
24. $9 \times 8 =$ ___

Find each quotient.

25. $48 \div 8 =$ ___
26. $27 \div 3 =$ ___
27. $54 \div 6 =$ ___
28. $45 \div 9 =$ ___
29. $16 \div 2 =$ ___
30. $40 \div 5 =$ ___

31. $28 \div 4 =$ ___
32. $56 \div 7 =$ ___
33. $12 \div 2 =$ ___
34. $32 \div 4 =$ ___
35. $42 \div 7 =$ ___
36. $63 \div 9 =$ ___

37. $24 \div 4 =$ ___
38. $9 \div 1 =$ ___
39. $64 \div 8 =$ ___
40. $35 \div 7 =$ ___
41. $36 \div 6 =$ ___
42. $8 \div 8 =$ ___

43. $81 \div 9 =$ ___
44. $24 \div 3 =$ ___
45. $49 \div 7 =$ ___
46. $72 \div 8 =$ ___
47. $45 \div 5 =$ ___
48. $18 \div 3 =$ ___

Check your answers on page 188.

Points to Remember

- Multiplication and division are opposite math operations.
- A multiplication answer is called a *product*; a division answer is called a *quotient*.
- Numbers can be multiplied in any order.
- When you multiply by 0 or divide into 0, the answer is 0.
- You cannot divide by zero.

Multiplication

You are setting up a room for a meeting. You need to make 4 equal rows with 6 chairs per row. How many chairs do you need altogether?

The problem asks you to find a total amount. By adding the number of chairs in each row four times, you can find the answer. Look at this picture. What is the total?

6 chairs in every row

4 equal rows

6 + 6 + 6 + 6 = _____

You need 24 chairs.

Another way to solve the problem is to use multiplication. Multiplication is the combining of equal groups to get a total. Fill in the missing numbers.

_____ × _____ = 24 ← total amount

number of times to combine the amount

amount you need to combine

You should have filled in 4 and 6.

Use addition to combine two or more amounts of the same thing.

6 chairs + 4 chairs = 10 chairs

Use multiplication to combine the *same* amount several times.

4 rows × 6 chairs per row = 24 chairs combined 4 times

In this chapter, you will study the basic skills you need to multiply numbers. You will practice using a calculator and estimating answers. You will also learn to use a strategy to solve real-life multiplication problems.

Solving Multiplication Problems

Read this problem.

> In one high school, the average class has **32 students**. A teacher teaches **3 classes** a day. About how many students does a teacher instruct each day?

To solve the problem, you can add 32 + 32 + 32, or you can multiply 32 by 3. The answer is **96 students**.

Multiplication problems are usually set up vertically. Line up the columns with ones under ones and tens under tens. Use a times sign (×) to show multiplication.

The two numbers you are multiplying can be written in any order, but it is easier to solve a multiplication problem if you put the number with fewer digits on the bottom. The number on the bottom is the **multiplier**. Multiply each digit in the top number by the multiplier.

First, multiply the ones digit in the top number by the multiplier. Then multiply the tens digit. Write the product for each column directly under the digits in that column. In the following problem, the multiplier is 3.

```
        tens ones
          ↓   ↓
          3   2      First multiply 3 by the digit in the ones: 3 × 2 = 6.
        ×     3      Then multiply 3 by the digit in the tens: 3 × 3 = 9.
product → 9   6      The product is 96.
```

The answer to a multiplication problem may have more digits than either of the numbers you multiplied together.

Multiply 4 × 91.

```
                    Rewrite the problem with 91 on top.
          9 1       First multiply 4 by the ones digit: 4 × 1 = 4.
        ×   4       Then multiply 4 by the tens digit: 4 × 9 = 36.
        3 6 4       The product is 364.
```

Notice that the digit 3 is in the hundreds column.

Exercise 1

Rewrite and solve each problem.

1. $3 \times 23 =$ 4. $3 \times 43 =$ 7. $72 \times 3 =$

2. $41 \times 2 =$ 5. $2 \times 64 =$ 8. $32 \times 4 =$

3. $12 \times 4 =$ 6. $9 \times 61 =$ 9. $5 \times 71 =$

Check your answers on page 188.

When one of the numbers in a multiplication problem has three digits, start by multiplying the ones digit in the top number by the multiplier. Then multiply the tens digit and finally the hundreds digit. The answer may have four digits.

Multiply 514×2.

$$\begin{array}{r} 5\,1\,4 \\ \times\quad 2 \\ \hline 1{,}0\,2\,8 \end{array}$$

Rewrite the problem with 514 on top.
First multiply 2 by the ones digit: $2 \times 4 = 8$.
Next multiply 2 by the tens digit: $2 \times 1 = 2$.
Then multiply 2 by the hundreds digit: $2 \times 5 = 10$.
The product is 1,028.

Exercise 2

Rewrite and solve each problem.

1. $4 \times 312 =$ 3. $522 \times 4 =$ 5. $2 \times 413 =$

2. $711 \times 5 =$ 4. $3 \times 912 =$ 6. $811 \times 5 =$

Check your answers on page 189.

Multiplying Zeros

Remember that a number multiplied by zero is always zero.

Find the product of 20 and 3.

$$\begin{array}{r} 20 \\ \times\ 3 \\ \hline 60 \end{array}$$

Write 20 on top.
Multiply 3 by the ones digit: $3 \times 0 = 0$.
Multiply 3 by the tens digit: $3 \times 2 = 6$.
The product is 60.

Exercise 3

Rewrite and solve each problem.

1. $40 \times 2 =$
2. $30 \times 3 =$
3. $7 \times 90 =$
4. $220 \times 4 =$
5. $3 \times 701 =$
6. $400 \times 2 =$
7. $810 \times 6 =$
8. $4 \times 502 =$

Check your answers on page 189.

On Your Calculator

Follow these steps to practice solving a multiplication problem on your calculator. Multiply 32 × 3.

1. Clear your calculator.
2. Enter the number being multiplied.
3. Press the times sign.
4. Enter the multiplier.
5. Press the equals sign.
6. Read the display.

C 3 2 × 3 = **96.**

Practice entering the problems in Exercises 1, 2, and 3 on your calculator.

Carrying in Multiplication

When the product of two digits is 10 or more, only one digit can go at the bottom of each column. If the product of the digits in the ones column is 10 or more, write the ones digit in the ones column. Then **carry** the tens digit to the next column.

After you find the product of the multiplier and the digit in the tens column, **add** the digit that you carried to the new product.

Read the examples carefully.

Multiply 39 by 2.

$$
\begin{array}{r}
1\ \ \ \\
39 \\
\times\ 2 \\
\hline
78
\end{array}
$$

Write 39 on top; the multiplier is 2.
Multiply 9 by 2: $2 \times 9 = 18$.
  Write 8 in the ones column and carry 1 to the tens.
Multiply 3 by 2: $2 \times 3 = 6$.
Add the 1 you carried to the product 6: $6 + 1 = 7$.
The answer is 78.

The answer may have more digits than either number in the problem.

Find the product of 7 and 56.

$$
\begin{array}{r}
4\ \ \ \\
56 \\
\times\ 7 \\
\hline
392
\end{array}
$$

Write 56 on top; the multiplier is 7.
Multiply 6 by 7: $7 \times 6 = 42$.
  Write 2 in the ones column and carry 4 to the tens.
Multiply 5 by 7: $7 \times 5 = 35$.
Add the 4 you carried to the product 35: $35 + 4 = 39$.
The product is 392.

Exercise 4

Solve each problem. Then check your work on a calculator. Redo incorrect problems.

1. $2 \times 27 =$ 3. $29 \times 3 =$ 5. $8 \times 72 =$ 7. $3 \times 57 =$

2. $45 \times 4 =$ 4. $63 \times 4 =$ 6. $46 \times 6 =$ 8. $68 \times 5 =$

Check your answers on page 189.

You may have to carry more than once. Read the next example carefully.

Multiply 293 by 7.

6 2
2 9 3
× 7
2,0 5 1

Write 293 on top; the multiplier is 7.
Multiply the ones: 7 × 3 = 21.
    Write 1 in the ones column and carry 2 to the tens.
Multiply the tens: 7 × 9 = 63.
Add the 2 you carried to the product 63: 63 + 2 = 65.
    Write 5 in the tens column and carry 6 to the hundreds.
Multiply the hundreds: 7 × 2 = 14.
Add the 6 you carried to the product 14: 14 + 6 = 20.
The answer is 2,051.

Multiply 3 × 108.

2
1 0 8
× 3
3 2 4

Multiply the ones: 3 × 8 = 24.
    Write 4 and carry 2.
Multiply the tens: 3 × 0 = 0 and add 2: 2 + 0 = 2.
    Write 2.
Multiply the hundreds: 3 × 1 = 3.
    Write 3.
The answer is 324.

When there is a zero in the number being multiplied, the product for that column is 0. If a digit was carried to that column, add the digit to zero.

Exercise 5

Solve each problem. Then check your work on a calculator. Redo incorrect problems.

1. 118 × 2 =   3. 4 × 278 =   5. 4 × 104 =   7. 409 × 3 =

2. 551 × 6 =   4. 8 × 392 =   6. 9 × 604 =   8. 6 × 807 =

Check your answers on page 189.

Two-Digit Multipliers

An electronics shop offers a payment plan for a 32-inch plasma TV: **$52 per month** for **24 months**. What is the total cost of the TV?

To solve the problem, multiply the monthly payment ($52) by the number of payments (24).

When you multiply by a two-digit number, you have to find two products and then add them. For the problem $52 × 24, either number can be the multiplier. If 24 is the multiplier, first calculate the **partial product** of 4 (the ones digit) times 52. Then calculate the partial product of 2 (the tens digit) times 52. The answer is the sum of the two partial products.

Follow each step in the example carefully. Notice how the partial products are lined up.

LANGUAGE Tip

Multiple Meanings

partial   PAR shuhl

Partial means "only part of the entire thing." We also use *partial* to mean "favoring one thing over another."

Example: I am partial toward chocolate ice cream.

What is $52 × 24?

```
  $  5 2
  ×  2 4
     2 0 8
   1 0 4
 $1,2 4 8
```

First multiply 4 by the ones digit: 4 × 2 = 8. Write 8.
Multiply 4 by the tens digit: 4 × 5 = 20. Write 20.
          The first partial product is 208.
Now multiply 2 by the ones digit: 2 × 2 = 4.
          Write 4 in the tens column.
Multiply 2 by the tens digit: 2 × 5 = 10. Write 10.
          The second partial product is 104.
Add the partial products. The answer is $1,248.

Exercise 6

1. 12 × 24 =

2. 13 × 32 =

3. 15 × 11 =

4. 24 × 21 =

5. 33 × 12 =

6. 21 × 48 =

Check your answers on page 189.

When you multiply by a two-digit number, you may have to carry digits. Again, read the example carefully. Notice how the partial products are lined up.

What is the product of 46 and 39?

$$\begin{array}{r} 46 \\ \times\ 39 \\ \hline 414 \\ 138 \\ \hline 1,794 \end{array}$$

First multiply 9 by the ones digit: $9 \times 6 = 54$.

Write 4 in the ones column and carry 5.

Multiply 9 by the tens digit: $9 \times 4 = 36$.

Add the 5 you carried to 36: $36 + 5 = 41$. Write 41.

The first partial product is 414.

Now multiply 3 by the ones digit: $3 \times 6 = 18$.

Write 8 in the tens column and carry 1.

Multiply 3 by the tens digit: $3 \times 4 = 12$.

Add the 1 you carried to 12: $12 + 1 = 13$. Write 13.

The second partial product is 138.

Add the partial products. The answer is 1,794.

Exercise 7

Solve each problem. Check your work with a calculator. Redo incorrect problems.

1. $27 \times 32 =$

2. $63 \times 45 =$

3. $85 \times 46 =$

4. $74 \times 58 =$

5. $93 \times 74 =$

6. $59 \times 37 =$

7. $84 \times 56 =$

8. $78 \times 19 =$

9. $209 \times 36 =$

10. $53 \times 905 =$

11. $17 \times 253 =$

12. $528 \times 46 =$

13. $73 \times 809 =$

14. $920 \times 85 =$

15. $367 \times 72 =$

16. $503 \times 89 =$

Check your answers on page 189.

Multiplying by 10, 100, and 1,000

Multiplication problems with two-digit multipliers are not always as complicated as the problems in the last three exercises.

Multiply 32 × 10.

$$\begin{array}{r} 3\,2 \\ \times\ 1\,0 \\ \hline 0\,0 \\ 3\,2 \\ \hline 3\,2\,0 \end{array}$$

Multiply $0 \times 2 = 0$. Write 0 in the ones column.
Multiply $0 \times 3 = 0$. Write 0 in the tens column.
Multiply $1 \times 2 = 2$. Write 2 in the tens column.
Multiply $1 \times 3 = 3$. Write 3 in the hundreds column.
The product is 320.

Notice that the answer to $32 \times 10 = 320$ is 32 with a zero (0) in the ones column. Multiplying by 100 and multiplying by 1,000 are also easy operations.

Math Note

- To multiply a number by 10, write a zero to the right of the number.

- To multiply a number by 100, write two zeros to the right of the number.

- To multiply a number by 1,000, write three zeros to the right of the number.

Look at these examples.

$$10 \times 19 = 190 \qquad 100 \times 287 = 28{,}700 \qquad 1{,}000 \times 36 = 36{,}000$$

Exercise 8

Write the answers and check your answers on a calculator. Redo incorrect problems.

1. $15 \times 10\ =$ _____
2. $28 \times 10\ =$ _____
3. $10 \times 365 =$ _____
4. $140 \times 10 =$ _____

5. $100 \times 9\ \ =$ _____
6. $31 \times 100\ =$ _____
7. $100 \times 78\ \ =$ _____
8. $239 \times 100 =$ _____

9. $58 \times 1{,}000\ =$ _____
10. $70 \times 1{,}000\ =$ _____
11. $1{,}000 \times 94\ \ =$ _____
12. $645 \times 1{,}000 =$ _____

Check your answers on page 189.

Multiplying by Tens, Hundreds, and Thousands

You have learned shortcuts for multiplying by 10, 100, and 1,000. Now you will learn shortcuts for multiplying by numbers that end with one or more zeros.

Earlier you learned that either number in a multiplication problem can be the multiplier. In these examples, you will see that the number that ends with one or more zeros is written as the multiplier even when it is larger than the other number.

Multiply 17 × 30.

```
    2
   1 7
 × 3 0
 5 1 0
```

Write 30 as the multiplier and bring down the zero.
Multiply 3 × 7 = 21; write 1 and carry 2.
Multiply 3 × 1 = 3 and add 2: 3 + 2 = 5.
The answer is 510.

Notice that the ones were not lined up in the example problem.

Multiply 200 × 34.

```
     3 4
 × 2 0 0
 6,8 0 0
```

Write 200 as the multiplier and bring down the two zeros.
Multiply 2 × 4 = 8.
Multiply 2 × 3 = 6.
The answer is 6,800.

Exercise 9

Solve each problem. Check your answers on a calculator. Redo incorrect problems.

1. 30 × 72 =
2. 96 × 80 =
3. 50 × 82 =
4. 600 × 7 =
5. 19 × 300 =
6. 347 × 200 =
7. 74 × 9,000 =
8. 4,000 × 60 =

Check your answers on page 189.

Estimated Products

To estimate a product, use rounded numbers. With a one-digit multiplier, round the larger number to the lead digit. Then find the product.

> Estimate 69 × 2.
>
> $$69 \approx 70 \qquad \text{Round 69 up to 70.}$$
> $$\underline{\times\ 2} \qquad \underline{\times\ 2} \qquad \text{Multiply: } 2 \times 70 = 140.$$
> $$\text{exact} \rightarrow 138 \approx 140 \leftarrow \text{estimate}$$

Exercise 10

Estimate by rounding the lead digit of the larger number. Then find the exact answer.

1. $43 \times 4 =$ 3. $9 \times 85 =$ 5. $3 \times 112 =$ 7. $185 \times 4 =$

2. $39 \times 6 =$ 4. $56 \times 7 =$ 6. $208 \times 2 =$ 8. $5 \times 326 =$

Check your answers on page 189.

To estimate a product with a two-digit multiplier, round each number to the lead digit.

> Estimate 18 × 84.
>
> $$84 \approx 80 \qquad \text{Round 84 down to 80.}$$
> $$\underline{\times\ 18} \approx \underline{\times\ 20} \qquad \text{Round 18 up to 20.}$$
> $$672 \qquad 1,600 \leftarrow \text{estimate}$$
> $$\underline{84}$$
> $$1,512 \leftarrow \text{exact}$$

Exercise 11

First estimate the answer by rounding to each lead digit. Then find the exact answer.

1. $18 \times 45 =$ 3. $27 \times 19 =$ 5. $56 \times 82 =$ 7. $289 \times 68 =$

2. $14 \times 72 =$ 4. $36 \times 24 =$ 6. $72 \times 36 =$ 8. $23 \times 392 =$

Check your answers on page 189.

Multiplication Word Problems

Use multiplication to solve real-life problems when you need to combine the same amount many times.

Read this example carefully to see how the strategy described in Chapter 4 can help you solve multiplication problems.

> A round-trip train ticket from Portland, Oregon, to Salinas, California, is $180. If you need 3 tickets, how much will you pay altogether?
>
> **1.** *State the problem in your own words.*
> Ask yourself, "What am I looking for?" For this problem, you might say, "I know the price of one ticket, and I need to calculate the price of 3 tickets."
>
> **2.** *List the facts.*
> What numbers do you need? In this problem, you have only two numbers: $180 for one ticket and 3 tickets.
>
> **3.** *Choose the mathematical operation you need.*
> You can add $180 three times or you can multiply $180 by 3.
>
> **4.** *Estimate the answer.*
> Round the lead digit to the nearest hundred. $180 ≈ $200.
> Multiply: $3 \times \$200 = \$600$. The answer should be *close to* $600.
>
> **5.** *Solve for the exact answer.*
> Use a calculator or solve the problem yourself.
>
> | 1 | 8 | 0 | × | 3 | = | 540. |
>
> The answer is **540.** You will pay $540 for three train tickets.

Exercise 12

For each problem, first estimate the answer by rounding the lead digit of every two-digit number and every three-digit number. Then find the exact answer. (Note: You will need an operation other than multiplication to solve at least one of the problems.)

1. Anna's share of rent is $425 per month. How much rent does she pay for 9 months?

Estimate	Exact

2. One serving of stir-fry beef contains 28 grams of protein. One gram of protein has 4 calories. How many protein calories are in one serving?

Estimate	Exact

3. Skip pays $101 per month for car insurance. He also pays $275 per month for his car loan. How much does he pay each month for the loan and the insurance?

Estimate	Exact

4. How much does Skip, in the last problem, pay for his loan and insurance in a full year? (1 year = 12 months)

Estimate	Exact

5. Carlos drives 38 miles to work each day. How many miles does Carlos travel in 5 work days driving to and from work?

Estimate	Exact

6. Mara can drive an average of 29 miles on one gallon of gasoline. Her tank holds 13 gallons. How many miles can she drive on a full tank of gas?

Estimate	Exact

Check your answers on page 189.

Points to Remember

- Begin a multiplication problem by multiplying the digit in the ones place of the multiplier by the digit in the ones place of the other number. Work from right to left.

- When a product has two number places, write the digit that is on the right. Carry the left digit to the next number place.

- Add any digit that you carried *after* multiplying the digits in that column.

- With a two-digit multiplier, first find the partial product for each digit. Then add the partial products to get the final answer.

Multiplication Checkup

Solve each problem.

1. $709 \times 6 =$

3. $503 \times 9 =$

5. $36 \times 100 \ =$

2. $8 \times 307 =$

4. $10 \times 73 =$

6. $1,000 \times 18 =$

First estimate each answer by rounding each lead digit and multiplying the rounded numbers. Then find the exact answers.

7. $57 \times 92 =$

Estimate	Exact

8. $83 \times 28 =$

Estimate	Exact

9. $312 \times 49 =$

Estimate	Exact

Solve each problem.

10. A sandwich shop sells a box lunch (sandwich, chips, drink, and dessert) for $4. Sam needs 48 lunches for his employees. What is the total cost?

11. Alice plans to ship 37 packages each of which weighs 12 pounds. Find the combined weight of the packages.

12. Barry can type 54 words per minute. He has 35 minutes to type a document that contains 2,000 words. Does he have enough time to type the document?

Check your answers on page 189.

Chapter 7

Division

A store has a sale on car engine oil. You and two friends buy a case of 24 quarts of oil. If you share the oil equally, how many quarts does each person get?

You need to find an equal amount per person. One way to figure out how many quarts each person will get is to pass out the quarts until none are left. This diagram represents the number of quarts each person will have.

24 quarts of oil separated into 3 equal groups. Each person gets 8 quarts of oil.

Another way to solve the problem is to use division. Division is separating a total into *equal* amounts. Fill in the missing numbers, using the amounts in the example.

$$\underline{\hspace{2cm}} \div \underline{\hspace{2cm}} = 8 \leftarrow \text{equal amount in each group}$$

    ↑   ↑

  total amount   number of equal groups

In this problem, you should have written **24** and **3**.

You use division to find the equal amount in each group. You can also use division to find the number of equal groups in a total amount.

Bill needs a part-time job. He can work only **24 hours** a week. If he works **8 hours** a day, how many days will he work each week?

$$24 \div 8 = 3 \text{ days} \leftarrow \text{number of equal groups}$$

     ↑ ↑

  total amount   equal amount in each group

In this chapter, you will study the basic skills for dividing numbers. You will practice using a calculator to find answers and use a strategy to solve real-life division problems.

Talk Math

Do this activity with a partner or a group.

1. Name situations in which you need to divide numbers.
2. Separate things in the classroom into equal groups.

Writing Division Problems

Read this problem.

> Kate's mother lives **86 miles** away. It takes **2 hours** for Kate to drive to her mother's house. At that rate, how far does Kate drive in one hour?

To get the answer, divide 86 by 2. The answer is 43.

When you divide, you find how many times a **divisor** goes into a **dividend**. The answer to a division problem is called the **quotient**.

The symbol ÷ means "divided by." Look at the labels for the numbers in the last problem.

> (the number to be divided) dividend → 86 ÷ 2 = 43 ← quotient (answer)
> ↑
> divisor (the number to divide by)

Another way to write a division problem is to use a division bracket $\overline{)}$. Again, look at the labels for the numbers in the last problem.

> 43 ← quotient (answer)
> 2)86 ← dividend (the number to be divided)
> ↑
> divisor (the number to divide by)

This problem can be read in two ways:
86 divided by 2   2 divided into 86
The answer is **43 miles**.

Exercise 1

For each pair of numbers, write two division problems. First use the ÷ sign. Then write the problem with the division bracket $\overline{)}$. Do not solve the problems.

1. 48 divided by 2
2. 39 divided by 6
3. 290 divided by 5
4. 8 divided into 248
5. 10 divided into 380
6. 96 divided by 32

Check your answers on page 189.

Solving Division Problems

When you solve a division problem, start by dividing into the digit at the left of the dividend. Continue working the problem from left to right.

Follow these steps.

1. *Divide* the first digit in the dividend by the divisor. Then write the quotient above that digit.

2. *Multiply* the quotient by the divisor. Then write the product under the digit you divided into.

3. *Subtract.*

4. *Bring down the next digit.*

Repeat the steps to divide into the next digit of the dividend.

Solve 2)78

```
         39
     2 )78        First:  Divide 7 ÷ 2 = 3 (but not evenly).
       - 6                Multiply 3 × 2 = 6.
         18               Subtract 7 − 6 = 1.
       - 18               Bring down the 8.
          0       Then:   Divide 18 ÷ 2 = 9.
                          Multiply 9 × 2 = 18.
                          Subtract 18 − 18 = 0.
```

You can check your answer by multiplying the quotient by the divisor. The answer should be the same as the dividend. For the example, $39 \times 2 = 78$.

Exercise 2

Finish solving these problems. Check your answers by multiplying. If any answer is not correct, redo the problem. The first one is done for you.

```
           48
 1.    2 )96
       - 8         48
         16       × 2
       - 16        96
          0      Check
```

3. 6)78

5. 2)82

2. 3)54

4. 4)92

6. 7)98

Check your answers on page 190.

Rewriting Division Problems

When a division problem is written with the ÷ symbol, the dividend is always written first—*before* the division sign. When a division problem is written with the $\overline{)}$ bracket, the dividend is always written inside the bracket.

Compare the two ways of writing a division problem.

$$86 \div 2 = 43 \leftarrow \text{quotient}$$
$$\uparrow \qquad \uparrow$$
$$\text{dividend} \qquad \text{divisor}$$

$$43 \leftarrow \text{quotient}$$
$$\text{divisor} \rightarrow 2\overline{)86} \leftarrow \text{dividend}$$

Exercise 3

Rewrite each problem using the division bracket $\overline{)}$. Solve and check the problems.

1. $95 \div 5 =$ 3. $91 \div 7 =$ 5. $92 \div 4 =$

2. $81 \div 3 =$ 4. $84 \div 6 =$ 6. $98 \div 2 =$

Check your answers on page 190.

On Your Calculator

Follow these steps to solve a division problem on your calculator.
Solve $86 \div 2$ on your calculator.

1. Clear your calculator.   3. Press the division sign.   5. Press the equals sign.

2. Enter the dividend.   4. Enter the divisor.   6. Read the display.

$$\boxed{C} \quad \boxed{8} \quad \boxed{6} \quad \boxed{\div} \quad \boxed{2} \quad \boxed{=} \quad \boxed{43.}$$

Practice entering the division problems in Exercises 2 and 3 on your calculator.

Uneven Division

Division problems do not always come out evenly. Read the next example carefully.

Solve $2\overline{)75}$

$$\begin{array}{r} 3\,7\ r\ 1 \\ 2\overline{)7\,5} \\ -\,6 \\ \hline 1\,5 \\ -\,1\,4 \\ \hline 1 \end{array}$$

First: Divide $7 \div 2 = 3$ (but not evenly).
Multiply $3 \times 2 = 6$.
Subtract $7 - 6 = 1$.
Bring down the 5.

Then: Divide $15 \div 2 = 7$ (but not evenly).
Multiply $7 \times 2 = 14$.
Subtract $15 - 14 = 1$.

The answer to the example is **37 remainder 1**. To check a division problem with a remainder, first multiply the quotient by the divisor. Then add the remainder.

$37 \times 2 = 74$ Then: $74 + 1 = 75$

Exercise 4

Rewrite each problem using the division bracket $\overline{)}$. Then solve and check each problem.

1. $83 \div 3 =$

2. $82 \div 6 =$

3. $97 \div 5 =$

4. $99 \div 8 =$

5. $95 \div 7 =$

6. $98 \div 3 =$

7. $70 \div 4 =$

8. $80 \div 6 =$

9. $88 \div 7 =$

Check your answers on page 190.

Note: If you use a calculator to solve an uneven division problem, the remainder is expressed as a decimal. We will study decimals in Unit 3 of this book.

Dividing into Three-Digit Numbers

To solve a division problem, you must divide, multiply, subtract, and bring down the next digit in the dividend. Repeat these steps until you have used each digit in the dividend.

This example shows how to use the steps to divide a three-digit dividend.

A washing machine costs **$656**. If Cheryl makes **4 equal payments**, how much will each payment be?

```
        1 6 4
    4 ) 6 5 6
      – 4
        2 5
      – 2 4
        1 6
      – 1 6
            0
```

First: Divide $6 \div 4 = 1$ (but not evenly).
Multiply $1 \times 4 = 4$, and subtract $6 - 4 = 2$.
Bring down the 5.

Then: Divide $25 \div 4 = 6$ (but not evenly).
Multiply $6 \times 4 = 24$, and subtract $25 - 24 = 1$.
Bring down the 6.

Then: Divide $16 \div 4 = 4$.
Multiply $4 \times 4 = 16$, and subtract $16 - 16 = 0$.

If Cheryl makes 4 equal payments, each payment will be **$164**.

Exercise 5

Rewrite each problem using the division bracket $\overline{)}$. Then solve and check each problem.

1. $635 \div 5 =$

2. $864 \div 4 =$

3. $768 \div 3 =$

4. $936 \div 8 =$

5. $774 \div 6 =$

6. $865 \div 4 =$

7. $784 \div 5 =$

8. $996 \div 7 =$

9. $935 \div 6 =$

Check your answers on page 190.

Cheryl, in the last example, decided to make **8 equal payments** for the $656 washing machine. How much will each payment be?

```
        8 2
    8 )6 5 6        First:  Divide 65 ÷ 8 = 8 (but not evenly).
    − 6 4                   Multiply 8 × 8 = 64, and subtract 65 − 64 = 1.
      1 6                   Bring down the 6.
    − 1 6          Then:    Divide 16 ÷ 8 = 2.
        0                   Multiply 2 × 8 = 16, and subtract 16 − 16 = 0.
```

If Cheryl makes 8 equal payments, each payment will be **$82**.

In this example, notice that the divisor 8 does not divide into the first digit in the dividend. We had to divide into the first two digits, 65.

Exercise 6

Rewrite each problem using the division bracket $\overline{)}$. Then solve and check each problem.

1. $581 \div 7 =$ 4. $354 \div 6 =$ 7. $349 \div 4 =$

2. $432 \div 8 =$ 5. $478 \div 7 =$ 8. $481 \div 9 =$

3. $378 \div 9 =$ 6. $468 \div 5 =$ 9. $429 \div 7 =$

Check your answers on page 190.

Zeros in Division Problems

After you write the first digit in a quotient, you need a digit in the quotient for every other digit in the dividend. Sometimes one of the digits in the dividend will be a zero.

Solve 206 ÷ 2.

$$
\begin{array}{r}
103 \\
2\overline{)206} \\
-2 \\
\hline
006 \\
-6 \\
\hline
0
\end{array}
$$

First: Divide 2 ÷ 2 = 1.
Multiply 1 × 2 = 2, and subtract 2 − 2 = 0.
Bring down the 0.

Then: Write a zero in the answer above the 0 you brought down.
Bring down the 6.

Then: Divide 6 ÷ 2 = 3.
Multiply 3 × 2 = 6, and subtract 6 − 6 = 0.
The quotient is **103**.

To check the example problem, multiply the quotient by the divisor. 103 × 2 = 206

Solve 452 ÷ 9.

$$
\begin{array}{r}
50\,r\,2 \\
9\overline{)452} \\
-45 \\
\hline
002 \\
-0 \\
\hline
2
\end{array}
$$

First: Divide 45 ÷ 9 = 5.
Multiply 5 × 9 = 45, and subtract 45 − 45 = 0.
Bring down the 2.

Then: Write a zero in the answer above the 2 you brought down.
Multiply 0 × 9 = 0, and subtract 2 − 0 = 2.
The quotient is **50 r 2**.

To check the example, multiply the quotient by the divisor and add the remainder.
50 × 9 = 450   Then: 450 + 2 = 452

Exercise 7

Rewrite each problem, using the division bracket $\overline{)}$. Solve and check each problem.

1. 604 ÷ 2 =
2. 960 ÷ 6 =
3. 355 ÷ 7 =
4. 480 ÷ 4 =
5. 425 ÷ 6 =
6. 913 ÷ 7 =

Check your answers on page 190.

Two-Digit Divisors

Dividing by a two-digit number requires some guessing. Sometimes you have to try more than one answer to solve a problem.

Think about the steps divide, multiply, subtract, and bring down the next digit. When you multiply a digit in the quotient by the divisor, the product should be smaller than or equal to the number you divided into. And when you subtract, the difference should be smaller than the divisor.

To guess a quotient, divide the first digit of the dividend by the first digit of the divisor.

Solve 72 ÷ 12.

$$\begin{array}{r} 7 \\ 12\overline{)72} \\ -84 \end{array}$$

Since 7 ÷ 1 = 7, try 7.
Multiply 12 × 7 = 84, but 84 is too large to subtract from 72.
The quotient is *not* 7.

$$\begin{array}{r} 5 \\ 12\overline{)72} \\ -60 \\ \hline 12 \end{array}$$

Since 7 is too large, try 5.
Multiply 12 × 5 = 60, and subtract 72 − 60 = 12.
Since the difference is 12, 5 is too small.
The quotient is *not* 5.

$$\begin{array}{r} 6 \\ 12\overline{)72} \\ -72 \\ \hline 0 \end{array}$$

Try 6.
Multiply 12 × 6 = 72, and subtract 72 − 72 = 0.
The quotient is **6**.

Exercise 8

Rewrite each problem, using the division bracket $\overline{)}$. Then solve and check each problem.

1. 68 ÷ 17 =

2. 182 ÷ 26 =

3. 120 ÷ 15 =

4. 312 ÷ 52 =

5. 115 ÷ 23 =

6. 130 ÷ 42 =

7. 450 ÷ 60 =

8. 580 ÷ 93 =

9. 300 ÷ 36 =

Check your answers on page 190.

More Two-Digit Divisors

In longer division problems, you can still guess a quotient by dividing the first digit of the dividend by the first digit in the divisor.

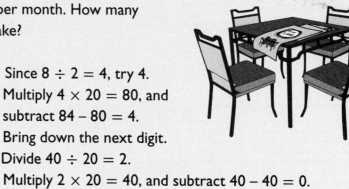

only $ 840

Mr. and Mrs. Garcia want to buy a dining room set for **$840**. They agree to pay **$20** per month. How many monthly payments will they make?

$$\begin{array}{r} 4\,2 \\ 20\,\overline{)8\,4\,0} \\ -\,8\,0 \\ \hline 4\,0 \\ -\,4\,0 \\ \hline 0 \end{array}$$

First: Since $8 \div 2 = 4$, try 4.
Multiply $4 \times 20 = 80$, and subtract $84 - 80 = 4$.
Bring down the next digit.

Then: Divide $40 \div 20 = 2$.
Multiply $2 \times 20 = 40$, and subtract $40 - 40 = 0$.
The quotient is **42**.

Mr. and Mrs. Garcia will make **42 monthly payments**.

Exercise 9

Rewrite each problem using the division bracket $\overline{)}$. Then solve and check each problem.

1. $270 \div 15 =$ 4. $1{,}558 \div 38 =$ 7. $1{,}053 \div 81 =$

2. $936 \div 13 =$ 5. $1{,}463 \div 19 =$ 8. $1{,}440 \div 45 =$

3. $598 \div 26 =$ 6. $1{,}080 \div 54 =$ 9. $2{,}914 \div 62 =$

Check your answers on page 190.

Estimating Quotients

One way to estimate a division problem is to use **compatible numbers**. Compatible numbers are numbers that divide evenly. These numbers are based on the basic division facts.

To use compatible numbers, first look at the divisor and the dividend. Ask yourself how you can change the problem so the numbers divide evenly and easily.

> Estimate the answer to $75 \div 9$.
> Think about a number that is close to 75 and can be divided evenly by 9.
> The closest number is 72.
>
> $$9 \overline{)75} \approx 9 \overline{)72} \qquad\qquad \begin{array}{r} 8 \leftarrow \text{Estimate} \\ 9 \overline{)72} \end{array} \text{The answer should be close to 8.}$$

A compatible dividend can be greater or smaller than the original dividend.

> Estimate the answer to $61 \div 7$.
> Think about numbers that are close to 61 and can be divided evenly by 7.
> Both 56 and 63 can be divided evenly by 7. The closest number is 63.
>
> $$7 \overline{)61} \approx 7 \overline{)63} \qquad\qquad \begin{array}{r} 9 \leftarrow \text{Estimate} \\ 7 \overline{)63} \end{array} \text{The answer should be close to 9.}$$

Exercise 10

Use compatible numbers to estimate each problem. The first problem is done as an example. Then find each exact answer.

1. $37 \div 6 \approx 36 \div 6$

2. $50 \div 7 \approx$ _____

3. $65 \div 9 \approx$ _____

4. $67 \div 8 \approx$ _____

5. $28 \div 3 \approx$ _____

6. $48 \div 5 \approx$ _____

7. $71 \div 9 \approx$ _____

8. $31 \div 4 \approx$ _____

9. $55 \div 8 \approx$ _____

10. $51 \div 7 \approx$ _____

Check your answers on page 190.

Estimating with Larger Numbers

When the dividend has three digits, try rounding to the **nearest compatible ten**.

Estimate the answer to $172 \div 6$.
Think about round numbers that are close to 172 and can be divided evenly by 6.
120, 150, and 180 can all be divided evenly by 6. The closest number is 180.

$$6 \overline{)172} \approx 6 \overline{)180}$$

$$\begin{array}{r} 30 \leftarrow \text{Estimate} \\ 6 \overline{)180} \end{array} \quad \text{The answer should be close to 30.}$$

Now solve the problem for the exact answer.

$$\begin{array}{r} 28\,r\,4 \\ 6 \overline{)172} \\ -12 \\ \hline 52 \\ -48 \\ \hline 4 \end{array}$$

The exact answer is close to the estimate of 30.

Exercise 11

Round each dividend to the nearest compatible ten to estimate each quotient. Then find the exact answers.

1. $258 \div 6 =$

2. $317 \div 8 =$

3. $163 \div 5 =$

4. $207 \div 3 =$

5. $468 \div 9 =$

6. $336 \div 7 =$

7. $425 \div 8 =$

8. $471 \div 6 =$

9. $612 \div 9 =$

Check your answers on page 190.

Estimating with Two-Digit Divisors

You may need to change both the divisor and the dividend to create a compatible pair. With a two-digit divisor, first round the divisor to the nearest ten. Then round the dividend to the **nearest compatible hundred**. Study the next example carefully.

LANGUAGE *Tip*

When reading directions, watch for words that tell you what steps to take. Underlining words such as *first, then,* and *after* will help you follow the directions.

Estimate the answer to 1,976 ÷ 38.

First round the divisor, 38, to the nearest ten. $38 \approx 40$

Think about round numbers that are close to 1,976 and can be divided evenly by 40.

Both 1,600 and 2,000 can be divided evenly by 40. The closer number is 2,000.

$$38\overline{)1,976} \approx 40\overline{)2,000} \qquad 40\overline{)2,000} \overset{50 \;\leftarrow \text{ Estimate}}{} \quad \text{The answer should be close to 50.}$$

Now solve the problem for the exact answer.

$$
\begin{array}{r}
52 \\
38\overline{)1,976} \\
-190 \\
\hline
76 \\
-76 \\
\hline
0
\end{array}
$$

The exact answer is close to the estimate of 50.

Exercise 12

To estimate these quotients, first round each divisor to the nearest ten. Then round the dividend to the nearest compatible hundred. After you find the estimate, calculate each exact answer.

1. $1,638 \div 39 \approx$ _____ **4.** $1,083 \div 18 \approx$ _____ **7.** $3,342 \div 72 \approx$ _____

2. $2,964 \div 52 \approx$ _____ **5.** $3,198 \div 39 \approx$ _____ **8.** $5,544 \div 88 \approx$ _____

3. $1,906 \div 23 \approx$ _____ **6.** $6,589 \div 57 \approx$ _____ **9.** $4,446 \div 57 \approx$ _____

Check your answers on page 190.

Solving Real-Life Division Problems

Review the steps of the strategy for solving word problems. Then practice some real-life division problems.

1. *State the problem in your own words.* What are you looking for?
2. *List the facts.* What numbers do you need?
3. *Choose the mathematical operation you need.* What do you do with the numbers?
4. *Estimate* so you know what a reasonable answer will be.
5. *Solve* for the exact answer. Use a calculator or solve the problem yourself.

Exercise 13

For each problem, first estimate an answer. Then find the exact answer.

1. A typing test lasted 6 minutes. Silvio typed 348 words within the time limit. What average number of words did he type per minute?

Estimate	Exact

2. A mattress factory gives a 60-month guarantee on its products. How many years does the guarantee last? (Note: 12 months = 1 year)

Estimate	Exact

3. Marla pays $95 each month on her car loan. How many months will she need to pay off the outstanding balance of $2,280?

Estimate	Exact

4. On a road map, 1 inch represents a distance of 35 miles. How far apart on the map are two cities that are actually 455 miles apart?

Estimate	Exact

5. A can of vegetable soup has 348 calories. If the can contains 4 servings, how many calories are in one serving?

Estimate	Exact

Check your answers on page 191.

Exercise 14

For each problem, first estimate an answer. Then find the exact answer.

1. Mark and his two brothers plan to share the cost of a used truck. The truck is on sale for $9,585. If the brothers share the cost equally, how much does each of them have to pay?

Estimate	Exact

2. A group of parents raised $1,638 for sports equipment at their children's school. Altogether 78 people contributed. What average amount did each person give?

Estimate	Exact

3. A freight elevator can carry a maximum weight of 2,000 pounds. If an engine weighing 983 pounds is placed on the elevator, how much more weight can the elevator carry?

Estimate	Exact

4. There are 22 classes in the Heywood elementary school. If there are 638 students registered at the school, what is the average number of students in each class?

Estimate	Exact

5. Jose's car gets an average of 28 miles per gallon. How far can he drive on a full tank that holds 12 gallons of gas?

Estimate	Exact

6. Last year Mr. and Mrs. Miller paid a total of $7,416 in rent. How much was their monthly rent?

Estimate	Exact

7. Lucy makes $648 a week at her job. Her boss is offering her a raise of $38 a week. How much will she make each week?

Estimate	Exact

Check your answers on page 191.

Points to Remember

- Be sure that the divisor and dividend are in the correct order.

- Divide the digits in the dividend from left to right.

- The steps for dividing the digits in a dividend are to *divide, multiply, subtract,* and *bring down the next digit.*

Division Checkup

Solve each problem.

1. $87 \div 3 =$

3. $266 \div 14 =$

5. $683 \div 17 =$

2. $90 \div 5 =$

4. $644 \div 28 =$

6. $1,253 \div 39 =$

First estimate each answer. Then find the exact answer.

7. $312 \div 6 =$

8. $266 \div 7 =$

9. $1,674 \div 62 =$

First estimate an answer. Then find the exact answer.

10. Sally's car used 28 gallons of gasoline to drive 588 miles. What is the average number of miles the car can travel on one gallon of gasoline?

Estimate	Exact

11. The Odeon movie theater has a total of 1,536 seats. Each row has 32 seats. How many rows of seats are in the theater?

Estimate	Exact

12. Jed drove 715 miles at an average speed of 55 mph. How many hours did he drive?

Estimate	Exact

Check your answers on page 191.

UNIT 2

Money

In this unit, you will learn the basic skills needed for working with money. You will learn how to

- express money in dollars, cents, and dollars-and-cents

- round money to the nearest dollar, dime, or penny

- add, subtract, multiply, and divide money

- estimate answers

- use a calculator to check your answers

Money Basics

LANGUAGE *Tip*

Most countries use a decimal system for their money.

Mexico I peso = 100 centavos

China I yuan = 10 jiao

Russia I ruble = 100 kopeks

India I rupee = 100 paisa

Every country has its own system of money. The basic unit of the money system in the United States is the **dollar**. The dollar sign (**$**) before a number indicates money.

A number system based on tens, hundreds, thousands, and so on is called a **decimal number system**. A decimal number system can express **parts** or **fractions** of a whole.

A **decimal point** separates whole amounts on the left of the decimal point from fractional amounts on the right of the decimal point. The digits to the right of the decimal point represent **dimes** (**tenths**) and **pennies** (**hundredths**). Together, the dimes place and the pennies place represent **cents** in our money system.

Whole dollar amounts can be shown with or without the number places for cents.

$$\$5 = \$5.00$$

Both expressions represent "five dollars." You can read the second expression as "five dollars *and* no cents."

Think about this amount: $14.26

We read $14.26 as "fourteen dollars and twenty-six cents." The digits 1 and 4 are in whole number places. They represent 14 whole dollars, or $14. The digits 2 and 6 are in the cents places. They represent 26 of the 100 equal parts in a dollar, or 26 cents.

As you work with dollars and cents in this unit, remember that you are working with decimals. (You will learn more about decimals in Unit 3.)

Talk Math

Do these activities with a partner or a group.

1. Make a list of situations in which you need to make calculations with money.
2. Take turns with a partner saying a dollar amount and telling a combination of bills that add up to that amount. For example, you might say, "$8." Your partner could say, "1 five-dollar bill and 3 one-dollar bills."

Number Places in Money

This chart shows the names of the first three whole number places in our money system. To the right of the decimal point are the two places that make up cents. (In decimals, the dimes place is called tenths, and the pennies place is called hundredths.)

The decimal point does not occupy a number place. It separates the whole number places on the left of the decimal point from the cents places on the right.

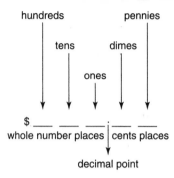

In $32.75,

> the digit 3 is in the tens place,
> the digit 2 is in the ones place,
> the digit 7 is in the dimes (or tenths) place
> the digit 5 is in the pennies (or hundredths) place

Exercise 1

1. In $7.59, which digit is in the pennies place? _____

2. In $30.14, which digit is in the tens place? _____

3. In $1.62, which digit is in the dimes place? _____

4. In $54.80, which two digits make the cents places? _____

5. In $9.17, the digit 1 is in what place? _____

6. In $63.49, the digit 6 is in what place? _____

7. In $0.58, the digit 8 is in what place? _____

8. In $17.30, the digit 0 is in what place? _____

9. In $10.99, the digit 0 is in what place? _____

Check your answers on page 191.

Place Value

Cents can be shown in two ways. One way is with the symbol (¢). The other is with a $ sign, a decimal point, and two number places. For example, 3¢ = $0.03 or $ .03.

Think about the most common coins in our number system.

one penny = 1¢ or $0.01 or $ .01   one quarter = 25¢ or $0.25 or $ .25
one nickel = 5¢ or $0.05 or $ .05   one half dollar = 50¢ or $0.50 or $ .50
one dime = 10¢ or $0.10 or $ .10

You learned in Chapter 1 that the placement of a digit in a whole number determines the digit's value. The same is true for the digits to the right of the decimal point.

> What is the value of each digit in $12.47?
>   The digit 1 is in the tens place. It has a value of 1 ten or $10.
>   The digit 2 is in the ones place. It has a value of $2.
>   The digit 4 is in the dimes place. It has a value of 4 × 10¢ = 40¢ or $0.40.
>   The digit 7 is in the pennies place. It has a value of 7¢ or $0.07.

Exercise 2

1. In $0.92, what is the value of the digit 9? _____

2. What is the value of the digit 6 in $8.56? _____

3. In $4.76, what is the value of the digit 4? _____

4. What is the value of the digit 3 in $0.31? _____

5. What is the value of the digit 4 in $346.12? _____

Check your answers on page 191.

On Your Calculator

When using a calculator for money problems, always use a decimal point before entering cents. To enter 38¢ (or $0.38) on your calculator, follow these steps.

1. Clear your calculator.   3. Enter the number.

2. Press the decimal point key.   4. Read the display.

C . 3 8 0.38

Money Place Value and Zeros

Think about these amounts.

$20.06 $20.60 $26.00

Each number has four number places.
Each number is written with just three digits: 0, 2, and 6.

The digit 0 has no value, but it keeps the other digits in their places.

Exercise 3

1. What is the value of the digit 6 in $20.06? _____

2. What is the value of the digit 6 in $20.60? _____

3. What is the value of the digit 6 in $26.00? _____

4. In $108.59, what is the value of the digit 1? _____

5. In $76.08, what is the value of the digit 8? _____

6. In $2.05, what is the value of the digit 5? _____

7. Which number has the *largest* digit in the dimes (tenths) place?
   a. $9.70   b. $8.60   c. $0.92   d. $24.08

8. Which number has the *smallest* digit in the pennies (hundredths) place?
   a. $10.14   b. $5.03   c. $30.56   d. $4.07

Check your answers on page 191.

 On Your Calculator

To enter $14.36 on a calculator, follow these steps.

1. Clear your calculator.   4. Enter the cents.

2. Enter the dollar amount.   5. Read the display.

3. Press the decimal point key.

(C) (I) (4) (.) (3) (6) (14.36)

Reading and Writing Dollars and Cents

Money amounts that are less than one dollar can be written two ways. You can use the ¢ symbol, or you can use the $ sign and a decimal point. In the examples, notice how zeros are used to hold number places.

> two cents = 2¢ or $0.02 or $ .02
> fifty cents = 50¢ or $0.50 or $ .50
> seventeen cents = 17¢ or $0.17 or $ .17

Exercise 4

Write each amount two ways, first with the ¢ symbol and digits and then with the $ sign, digits, and a decimal point.

1. five cents _____ _____
2. ten cents _____ _____
3. thirteen cents _____ _____
4. eighty cents _____ _____

5. forty cents _____ _____
6. nine cents _____ _____
7. fifty-four cents _____ _____
8. seventy-nine cents _____ _____

Check your answers on page 191.

A decimal point separates dollars from cents. When we read money amounts, the word *and* separates the whole dollar amount from the cents amount.

> Write nineteen dollars and eighty-two cents with a $ sign, digits, and a decimal point. Write 19 to the left of the decimal point and 82 to the right.
> $19.82

Exercise 5

Write each amount with a $ sign, digits, and a decimal point.

1. five dollars and twenty cents _____
2. sixteen dollars and nine cents _____
3. three dollars and forty-one cents _____

4. seven dollars and fifty cents _____
5. forty dollars and eight cents _____
6. twelve dollars and thirty cents _____

Check your answers on page 191.

Rounding to the Nearest Dollar

When we talk about money, we often round to the nearest dollar. Instead of saying that a shirt costs $24.95, we say that it costs $25.

To round to the nearest dollar, look at the digit to the right of the ones place. This is the dimes place.

> If the digit in the dimes place is less than 5, round down.
> If the digit in the dimes place is 5 or more, round up.

Round $24.95 to the nearest dollar.
    Since the digit to the right of the ones is 9, round up. $24.95 ≈ $25 or $25.00

Round $16.45 to the nearest dollar.
    Since the digit to the right of the ones is 4, round down. $16.45 ≈ $16 or $16.00

Round $49.83 to the nearest dollar.
    Since the digit to the right of the ones is 8, round up.
    To round up, add 1 to 49. $49.83 ≈ $50 or $50.00

Exercise 6

Round each amount to the nearest dollar.

1. $5.92 ≈ _____
2. $3.18 ≈ _____
3. $12.05 ≈ _____

4. $25.47 ≈ _____
5. $74.60 ≈ _____
6. $89.59 ≈ _____

7. $32.09 ≈ _____
8. $19.85 ≈ _____
9. $128.72 ≈ _____

Use $208.76 to answer questions 10–12.

10. Round the amount to the nearest dollar. _____
11. Round the amount to the nearest ten dollars. _____
12. Round the amount to the nearest hundred dollars. _____

Check your answers on page 191.

Rounding to the Nearest Dime

To round to the nearest dime, look at the digit to the right of the dimes place. This is the pennies place.

If the digit in the pennies place is less than 5, round down.

If the digit in the pennies place is 5 or more, round up.

Then write a 0 in the pennies place.

Round $0.13 to the nearest dime.
Since the digit to the right of the dimes is 3, round down. $0.13 ≈ $0.10

Round $2.65 to the nearest dime.
Since the digit to the right of the dimes is 5, round up. $2.65 ≈ $2.70

Round $6.98 to the nearest dime.
Since the digit to the right of the dimes is 8, round up.
To round up, add 1 to 9 and carry to the ones. $6.98 ≈ $7.00

Exercise 7

Round each amount to the nearest dime.

1. $0.45 ≈ _____
2. $0.06 ≈ _____
3. $0.81 ≈ _____

4. $0.75 ≈ _____
5. $1.98 ≈ _____
6. $1.23 ≈ _____

7. $4.48 ≈ _____
8. $5.37 ≈ _____
9. $8.96 ≈ _____

Use $12.58 to answer questions 10–12.

10. Round the amount to the nearest dime. _____

11. Round the amount to the nearest dollar. _____

12. Round the amount to the nearest ten dollars. _____

Check your answers on page 191.

Rounding to the Nearest Penny

You may see money written with three decimal places. For example, the price of a gallon of gasoline is often written with three decimal places. You can round this amount to the nearest penny.

To round to the nearest penny, look at the digit to the right of the pennies place. (The third place to the right of the decimal point is the thousandths.)

If the digit to the right of the pennies place is less than 5, round down.

If the digit to the right of the pennies place is 5 or more, round up.

> Round $1.236 to the nearest penny.
> Since the digit to the right of the pennies place is 6, round up. $1.236 ≈ $1.24
>
> Round $2.974 to the nearest penny.
> Since the digit to the right of the pennies place is 4, round down. $2.974 ≈ $2.97

Exercise 8

Round each amount to the nearest penny. (Remember to write the $ sign in your answer.)

1. $0.188 ≈ _____
2. $0.453 ≈ _____
3. $0.094 ≈ _____

4. $0.915 ≈ _____
5. $1.473 ≈ _____
6. $2.139 ≈ _____

7. $3.604 ≈ _____
8. $2.508 ≈ _____
9. $5.999 ≈ _____

Check your answers on page 191.

Points to Remember

• The decimal point separates dollar amounts on the left from the cents on the right.

• Dollar amounts have the same place values as whole numbers (ones, tens, hundreds, and so on).

• Cents have two decimal places: dimes (tenths) and pennies (hundredths).

Money Checkup

Use $256.19 to answer questions 1–3.

1. The digit 5 is in what number place? _____
2. The digit 1 is in what number place? _____
3. The digit 9 is in what number place? _____

Answer the questions.

4. What is the value of the digit 4 in $38.47? _____
5. What is the value of the digit 6 in $2.76? _____
6. What is the value of the digit 5 in $53.07? _____

Use numbers and symbols to write the amounts.

7. four cents _____
8. eighty-five cents _____
9. one dollar and thirteen cents _____
10. twenty dollars and seven cents _____
11. four dollars and thirty cents _____
12. seventeen dollars and sixty-one cents _____

Answer the questions.

13. Round $8.39 to the nearest dollar. _____
14. Round $46.75 to the nearest dime. _____
15. Round $3.198 to the nearest penny. _____

Check your answers on page 191.

Chapter 9

Calculating with Money

We solve money problems every day. Read the following questions. Decide whether you would add, subtract, multiply, or divide to answer each question. Then explain why you chose that operation.

1. Melvin earns $8.60 per hour. How much does he earn for 40 hours of work?

2. Last month the Wilsons paid $27.15 for garbage pickup, $22.83 for water, and $46.94 for electricity. How much were their house bills for the month?

3. A microwave oven costs $139.99. If the price is reduced by $20.00, how much will it cost?

4. A monthly bus pass costs $70. If you use the pass for 40 bus rides, how much will each bus ride cost?

Questions **1** and **2** ask for total amounts. To answer question **1**, multiply $8.60 by 40. To answer question **2**, add the three amounts.

Question **3** asks for a difference. To answer question **3**, subtract $20.00 from $139.99.

Question **4** asks for equal parts of a total amount. To answer question **4**, divide $70 by 40.

Talk Math

Do these activities with a partner or a group.
1. Describe real-life situations in which you calculate with money. What operation would you use in each situation?
2. With a partner, practice drilling the basic addition, subtraction, multiplication, and division facts.

Adding Money

When you add whole dollar amounts, first line up the numbers with ones under ones, tens under tens, and so on.

Find the sum of $657 and $86.
Write the problem with ones under ones and tens under tens.

    1 1
$ 6 5 7   Add the ones: $7 + 6 = 13$.
+   8 6   Write 3 under the ones column and carry 1 to the tens.
$ 7 4 3   Add the tens: $1 + 5 + 8 = 14$.
                     Write 4 under the tens and carry 1 to the hundreds.
                Add the hundreds: $1 + 6 = 7$. The sum is $743.

Exercise 1

Solve each problem. Check your answers on a calculator. Redo incorrect problems.

1. $55 + $179 =   3. $71 + $485 =   5. $347 + $21 + $165 =

2. $577 + $88 =   4. $106 + $95 =   6. $270 + $843 + $79 =

Check your answers on page 192.

When you add cents, line up the decimal points. Write pennies under pennies, dimes under dimes, and dollars under dollars.

Find the sum of $2.39 + $0.42 + $0.78.
Rewrite the numbers with pennies under pennies, dimes under dimes, and dollars under dollars.

    1 1
$ 2.3 9   Add the pennies: $9 + 2 + 8 = 19$. Write 9 and carry 1.
   0.4 2   Add the dimes: $1 + 3 + 4 + 7 = 15$. Write 5 and carry 1.
+ 0.7 8   Add the ones: $1 + 2 = 3$. The sum is $3.59
$ 3.5 9

Exercise 2

Solve each problem. Then check your answers. (To review entering money on a calculator, reread page 79.) If any answer is not correct, redo the problem.

1. $4.35 + $0.82 =   **3.** $2.70 + $8.90 =   **5.** $0.64 + $2.58 + $4.06 =

2. $0.60 + $3.47 =   **4.** $6.18 + $0.85 =   **6.** $4.98 + $3.86 + $0.72 =

Check your answers on page 192.

Math Note

A whole dollar amount is understood to have a decimal point at the right end. $5 is the same as $5.00.

Exercise 3

First estimate each answer by rounding the numbers to the nearest dollar and adding the rounded numbers. Then find the exact answers.

1. $1.20 + $5.19 =   **4.** $3.08 + $9.27 =   **7.** $10.47 + $6.92 + $7 =

2. $4.23 + $3.56 =   **5.** $2.46 + $5.86 =   **8.** $9 + $10.98 + $28.69 =

3. $5.46 + $6.42 =   **6.** $9.99 + $8.05 =   **9.** $22.35 + $5 + $10.75 =

Check your answers on page 192.

Math Note

If the answer in the pennies place is zero, most calculators will show the answer only to the dimes place. For example, the answer "$1.20" will appear as "1.2" on a calculator.

Subtracting Money

To subtract money, line up the decimal points. Write pennies under pennies, dimes under dimes, and dollars under dollars.

When a zero fills a column, you cannot borrow from it. To borrow 1, go to the next column to the left that is not a zero. In the following example, the first digit you can borrow from is in the ones place.

Subtract $5 – $0.82.   Rewrite $5 as $5.00.
    9   Borrow 1 from 5. Now there are 4 ones.
  4 ⅩΦ10   Add the 1 to the 0 in the dimes column:
$ 5.Φ Φ   1 dollar + 0 dimes = 10 dimes.
– 0.8 2   Next borrow 1 dime from the 10 dimes. Now there are 9 dimes.
$ 4.1 8   Add the 1 dime to the 0 in the pennies column: 10 + 0 = 10 pennies.
           Subtract the new pennies: 10 – 2 = 8.
           Subtract the new dimes: 9 – 8 = 1.
           Subtract the new ones: 4 – 0 = 4.
           The answer is $4.18.

Exercise 4

Solve each problem. Check your answers on a calculator. Redo incorrect problems.

1. $1 – $0.18 =   2. $10 – $2.36 =   3. $5 – $4.68   =

Estimate each answer by rounding the numbers to the nearest dollar and subtracting the rounded numbers. Then find the exact answers.

4. $6.36 – $1.26 =   7. $7.53 – $2.09 =   10. $16 – $2.45   =

5. $8.49 – $3   =   8. $19.38 – $5.29 =   11. $38.52 – $4.88 =

6. $12.66 – $10.15 =   9. $14.72 – $10.45 =   12. $17.06 – $10.77 =

Check your answers on page 192.

Multiplying Money

When you multiply money, you can write the two numbers in any order. However, it is easier to solve a multiplication problem if you put the number with fewer digits on the bottom.

The number on the bottom is the **multiplier**. Multiply the multiplier by each digit in the top number.

Find the product of $37 × 8.

5	Rewrite the problem with $37 on top.
$ 3 7	Multiply 8 × 7 = 56; write 6 and carry 5.
× 8	Multiply 8 × 3 = 24, and add 5: 24 + 5 = 29.
$2 9 6	The product is $296.

Exercise 5

Solve each problem. You can check your answers on a calculator. If any answer is not correct, redo the problem.

1. $612 × 8 =

2. 6 × $127 =

3. $260 × 9 =

4. $7 × 208 =

5. 3 × $485 =

6. $299 × 4 =

First estimate each answer by rounding the larger number to the lead digit and multiplying with the rounded number. (To review rounding to a lead digit, reread page 26.) Then find the exact answers.

7. $375 × 2 =

8. $9 × 260 =

9. 7 × $807 =

10. 512 × $6 =

11. 8 × $691 =

12. 418 × $4 =

Check your answers on page 192.

Multiplying Cents

To multiply dollars and cents, put the decimal point in the answer between the ones place and the dimes place.

Find the product of 4 × $7.68.

```
    2 3
 $ 7.6 8
   ×  4
 $3 0.7 2
```

Rewrite the problem with $7.68 on top.
Multiply 4 × 8 = 32. Write 2 and carry 3.
Multiply 4 × 6 = 24, and add 3: 24 + 3 = 27.
  Write 7 and carry 2.
Multiply 4 × 7 = 28, and add 2: 28 + 2 = 30.
Write a decimal point between the ones and dimes places.
The product is $30.72.

Exercise 6

Solve each problem, and check your answers. Redo incorrect problems.

1. $0.39 × 3 =   3. $0.47 × 9 =   5. $0.90 × 8 =

2. 7 × $0.58 =   4. 6 × $0.78 =   6. 4 × $0.96 =

First estimate each answer. Then find the exact answer.

7. 8 × $5.63 =   9. 5 × $7.06 =   11. 8 × $6.08 =

8. $6.98 × 4 =   10. $9.40 × 7 =   12. $7.53 × 6 =

Check your answers on page 192.

Two-Digit Multipliers

In Unit 1, you learned how to multiply when the multiplier has two digits. Use the same steps when you need to multiply a dollar amount by a two-digit multiplier. (To review two-digit multipliers, reread pages 51–52.)

Carmen earns $9.70 an hour. How much does she make in a week when she works 35 hours?

$$
\begin{array}{r}
\$9.70 \\
\times\ 35 \\
\hline
4850 \\
2910\ \\
\hline
\$339.50
\end{array}
$$

First multiply 5 by the pennies digit: $5 \times 0 = 0$. Write 0.
Multiply 5 by the dimes digit: $5 \times 7 = 35$. Write 5 and carry 3.
Multiply 5 by the ones digit: $5 \times 9 = 45$, and add 3. $45 + 3 = 48$.
 The first partial product is 4850.
Now multiply 3 by the pennies digit: $3 \times 0 = 0$.
Multiply 3 by the dimes digit: $3 \times 7 = 21$. Write 1 and carry 2.
Multiply 3 by the ones digit: $3 \times 9 = 27$, and add 2. $27 + 2 = 29$.
 The second partial product is 2910.
Add the partial products.
Count two places from the right for the decimal point.
Carmen makes $339.50 for a week's work.

Exercise 7

Solve these problems. Check your answers on a calculator. Redo incorrect problems.

1. $16 \times \$42 =$

2. $\$67 \times 25 =$

3. $\$48 \times 24 \ \ =$

4. $36 \times \$0.75 =$

5. $\$0.90 \times 58 =$

6. $27 \times \$1.05 =$

First estimate each answer by rounding to the nearest dollar. Find the product with the rounded dollar amount. Then find each exact answer.

7. $28 \times \$1.79 =$

8. $\$6.08 \times 14 =$

9. $\$9.82 \times 25 =$

10. $31 \times \$7.26 =$

11. $47 \times \$4.13 =$

12. $\$1.88 \times 53 =$

Check your answers on page 192.

Dividing Money

To divide money, follow the same steps you used for dividing whole numbers. (To review dividing, reread pages 61–68.) When you want to find the answer in both dollars and cents, add two zeroes to the dollar amount and continue dividing. Place the decimal point in your answer directly over the decimal point in the dividend.

Find the quotient of $15 ÷ 4.

```
   $  3.7 5
4 )$1 5.0 0
   - 1 2
      3 0
    - 2 8
      2 0
    - 2 0
        0
```

First: Rewrite $15 as $15.00, and bring up the decimal point.
Then: Divide 15 ÷ 4 = 3 with a remainder.
Multiply 3 × 4 = 12, and subtract 15 − 12 = 3.
Bring down the 0.
Then: Divide 30 ÷ 4 = 7 with a remainder.
Multiply 7 × 4 = 28, and subtract 30 − 28 = 2.
Bring down the next 0.
Then: Divide 20 ÷ 4 = 5.
Multiply 5 × 4 = 20, and subtract 20 − 20 = 0.
The quotient is $3.75.

Exercise 8

Solve each problem. Use a calculator to check the quotient. Redo incorrect problems.

1. $9 ÷ 2 =
2. $17 ÷ 4 =
3. $18 ÷ 5 =
4. $23 ÷ 2 =
5. $39 ÷ 4 =
6. $52 ÷ 8 =
7. $76 ÷ 8 =
8. $96 ÷ 5 =
9. $42 ÷ 8 =
10. $65 ÷ 4 =
11. $47 ÷ 5 =
12. $54 ÷ 4 =

Check your answers on page 192.

When you divide money, place the decimal point in your answer directly above the decimal point in the dividend.

What is $17.94 ÷ 3?

```
    $ 5.9 8    First:  Write a decimal point above its place in the dividend.
3 )$1 7.9 4    Then:   Divide 17 ÷ 3 = 5 with a remainder.
  - 1 5                Multiply 5 × 3 = 15, and subtract 17 − 15 = 2.
    2 9               Bring down the 9.
  - 2 7        Then:   Divide 29 ÷ 3 = 9 with a remainder.
    2 4                Multiply 9 × 3 = 27, and subtract 29 − 27 = 2.
  - 2 4                Bring down the 4.
      0      Then:   Divide 24 ÷ 3 = 8.
                       Multiply 3 × 8 = 24, and subtract 24 − 24 = 0.
                       The quotient is $5.98.
```

Exercise 9

Solve each problem. Use a calculator to check the quotient. Redo incorrect problems.

1. $6.15 ÷ 3 =

2. $9.04 ÷ 2 =

3. $16.60 ÷ 4 =

4. $19.80 ÷ 6 =

5. $39.45 ÷ 5 =

6. $50.24 ÷ 8 =

7. $69.93 ÷ 7 =

8. $26.64 ÷ 12 =

9. $40.32 ÷ 24 =

10. $71.20 ÷ 20 =

11. $129 ÷ 15 =

12. $361.80 ÷ 10 =

Check your answers on page 192.

Math Note

When dividing money, you need a digit in both the dimes and pennies places. If the divisor is larger than a digit in the dividend, write zero (0) in the quotient.

```
      $0.0 8
3 )$0.2 4
    - 2 4
        0
```

Rounding Remainders

If you have a remainder after dividing the pennies place, write a zero (0) in the third decimal place of the dividend. (The third decimal place is called *thousandths*.) Then divide into the new decimal place. Round your answer to the nearest penny.

> To the nearest penny, what is the quotient of $0.59 ÷ 5?
>
> ```
>        $0.1 1 8
>    5 )$0.5 9 0      ←—— Add a zero after the pennies place.
>      - 5
>        0 9
>      -   5
>          4 0
>        - 4 0
>            0
> ```
>
> Since the digit to the right of the pennies is 8, round $0.118 up to $0.12.

Exercise 10

Solve each problem, and round the quotient to the nearest penny. You can check your answer on a calculator. (Note: Round the calculator answers to the nearest penny.) If any answer is not correct, redo the problem.

1. $0.66 ÷ 8 =

2. $0.81 ÷ 6 =

3. $0.90 ÷ 7 =

4. $4.53 ÷ 2 =

5. $5.17 ÷ 3 =

6. $17.75 ÷ 7 =

7. $38.09 ÷ 6 =

8. $29.68 ÷ 5 =

9. $50.90 ÷ 8 =

10. $82.71 ÷ 4 =

11. $96.34 ÷ 9 =

12. $99.03 ÷ 7 =

Check your answers on pages 192–193.

Estimating Quotients

Division is the most difficult of the four basic operations. Estimating division answers is more difficult than estimating answers to addition, subtraction, and multiplication problems. To decide whether the answer to a division problem is reasonable, it is a good idea to estimate the quotient.

Estimate the answer to $4.32 ÷ 6. Then solve for the exact answer.
Think about round numbers that are close to $4.32 and can be divided evenly by 6.
$3.60, $4.20, and $4.80 can all be divided evenly by 6. The closest number is $4.20.

$$6\overline{)\$4.32} \approx 6\overline{)\$4.20}$$

$$\begin{array}{r} \$0.70 \quad \longleftarrow \text{Estimate} \\ 6\overline{)\$4.20} \end{array} \quad \text{The answer should be close to } \$0.70.$$

$$\begin{array}{r} \$0.7\,2 \\ 6\overline{)\$4.3\,2} \end{array} \quad \text{The exact answer is close to the estimate of } \$0.70.$$

Exercise 11

First estimate each answer. Then find the exact answer.

1. $5.44 ÷ 8 =

2. $3.24 ÷ 6 =

3. $4.10 ÷ 5 =

4. $4.13 ÷ 7 =

5. $8.28 ÷ 9 =

6. $3.92 ÷ 4 =

7. $56.52 ÷ 9 =

8. $34.44 ÷ 7 =

9. $169.04 ÷ 8 =

10. $58.74 ÷ 6 =

11. $33.44 ÷ 4 =

12. $59.25 ÷ 5 =

Check your answers on page 193.

Money Word Problems

Review the strategy for solving word problems on page 72.

Exercise 12

For each problem, first estimate an answer. Then find the exact answer.

1. One month Maria paid $37.92 for electricity and $61.85 for telephone service. What was the total of these utility bills?

Estimate	Exact

2. Frank bought groceries for a total of $72.56. He paid with $80. How much change did he receive?

Estimate	Exact

3. Julia makes $12.75 an hour as an electrician's assistant. How much does she make in a day when she works 8 hours?

Estimate	Exact

4. A class of school children sold $572 worth of tickets for their play. If they sold a total of 88 tickets, what was the price of one ticket?

Estimate	Exact

5. Silvia bought a gallon of milk for $2.59, a pound of cheese for $4.99, and a loaf of bread for $1.29. How much did she pay altogether for these items?

Estimate	Exact

Check your answers on page 193.

Points to Remember

- To add or subtract money, line up the decimal points. Write dollars under dollars, dimes under dimes, and pennies under pennies.

- To multiply money, count two places from the right in the answer to place the decimal point.

- To divide into money, place the decimal point in the answer directly above its position in the dividend.

Money Checkup

First estimate for each problem. Then find the exact answer.

1. $12.56 + $7.68 =

2. $3.24 + $14.79 =

3. $65.73 − $29.89 =

4. 8 × $7.35 =

5. $9.55 ÷ 5 =

6. $80.76 ÷ 3 =

7. 38 × $4.09 =

8. $60 − $49.27 =

9. $8.12 × 4 =

Round each number to the nearest penny.

10. $14.666 = _____

11. $5.333 = _____

First estimate each answer. Then find the exact answer.

12. One gallon of paint costs $17.99. If Bill needs 3 gallons, what is the total cost?

Estimate	Exact

13. At the drugstore, Amy's total purchases were $11.67. If she gave the cashier $20.07, how much change did she get back?

Estimate	Exact

14. The Johnsons pay $618.55 a month for rent and $127.50 for their car loan. What is the combined amount they pay for these expenses?

Estimate	Exact

15. Andy makes $494 for a week when he works 40 hours. How much does he make each hour?

Estimate	Exact

Check your answers on page 193.

Decimals

In this unit, you will learn the basic skills needed for working with decimals. You will learn how to

- identify decimal places and their values

- recognize decimals that have the same value

- compare decimals

- round decimals

- add, subtract, multiply, and divide decimals

- estimate answers

- use a calculator to solve decimal problems

Decimal Basics

We use cents to describe parts of a dollar. We use **decimals** to describe parts of a whole number.

$0.56 represents 56 of the 100 equal parts in a dollar.

0.3 represents 3 of the 10 equal parts in the number 1.

0.20 represents 20 of the 100 equal parts in the number 1.

0.625 represents 625 of the 1,000 equal parts in the number 1.

In Unit 2, you learned that we use decimals whenever we deal with money. We also use decimals to measure length, distance, weight, and temperature.

The pictures below show some measuring scales that you are probably familiar with. Look at each scale. Then tell whether the scale is used to measure weight, distance, or volume.

Scale A measures _____

Scale B measures _____

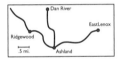

Scale C measures _____

Notice that all three scales show decimals. Scale A measures **weight**, scale B measures **distance**, and scale C measures **volume**.

Talk Math

Do these activities with a partner or a group.

1. Make a list of items in your purse or wallet that have decimals written on them.

2. With a partner, take turns naming a type of measure and having your partner respond with an appropriate unit of measurement. For example, you might say, "Weight." Your partner could respond, "Pounds."

Understanding Decimals

The digits to the right of a decimal point are called **decimals**. They represent parts of the number 1. Decimals divide the number 1 into tenths, hundredths, thousandths, and so on.

Decimals get their names from the number of places to the right of the decimal point.

The first place to the right of the decimal point is **tenths**.

The second place to the right of the decimal point is **hundredths**.

The third place to the right of the decimal point is **thousandths**.

> This box is divided into **10** equal parts, and **7** parts are shaded. The decimal **0.7** (seven tenths) represents the part of the box that is shaded.

Exercise 1

For each problem, fill in the blanks to describe the box.

1. a. The box is divided into _____ equal parts, and _____ parts are shaded.

   b. The decimal _____ represents the part of the box that is shaded.

2. a. The box is divided into _____ equal parts, and _____ parts are shaded.

   b. The decimal _____ represents the part of the box that is shaded.

3. a. The box is divided into _____ equal parts, and _____ parts are shaded.

   b. The decimal _____ represents the part of the box that is shaded.

4. a. The box is divided into _____ equal parts, and _____ parts are shaded.

   b. The decimal _____ represents the part of the box that is shaded.

Check your answers on page 193.

Decimal Place Value

This chart shows the names of the first four whole number places in our number system. To the right of the decimal point are the names of the first three decimal places.

The decimal point does not occupy a number place. It separates the whole number places on the left from the decimal places on the right.

The value of each place gets smaller (10 times smaller) as you move from left to right.

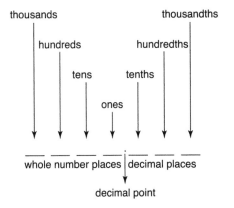

Think about this number.   0.157

The digit 1 is in the tenths place. It has value of 1 tenth, or 0.1.
The digit 5 is in the hundredths place. It has a value of 5 hundredths, or 0.05.
The digit 7 is in the thousandths place. It has a value of 7 thousandths, or 0.007.
In 0.157, the digit with the greatest value is 1.

Exercise 2

Use the number 0.249 to answer questions 1–5.

1. Which digit is in the tenths place? _____

2. The digit 4 represents 4 of the _____ equal parts of 1.

3. The digit 9 is in which place? _____

4. The digit 2 represents 2 of the _____ equal parts of 1.

5. Which digit in 0.249 has the greatest value? _____

Use the number 0.537 to answer questions 6–10.

6. Which digit is in the thousandths place? _____

7. The digit 5 represents 5 of the _____ equal parts of 1.

8. The digit 3 is in which place? _____

9. The digit 3 represents 3 of the _____ equal parts of 1.

10. Which digit in 0.537 has the greatest value? _____

Check your answers on page 193.

Reading and Writing Decimals

A decimal gets its name from the last decimal place. Read these examples carefully.

> Read 0.27 as "twenty-seven **hundredths**," since the last decimal place is hundredths.
> Read 0.6 as "six **tenths**," since the last decimal place is tenths.
> Read 0.004 as "four **thousandths**," since the last decimal place is thousandths.

Exercise 3

For each problem, fill in the blank to complete the name of the decimal.

1. 0.15 = fifteen _____
2. 0.106 = one hundred six _____
3. 0.9 = nine _____
4. 0.08 = eight _____
5. 0.013 = thirteen _____

6. 0.027 = twenty-seven _____
7. 0.64 = sixty-four _____
8. 0.1 = one _____
9. 0.206 = two hundred six _____
10. 0.009 = nine _____

Check your answers on page 193.

In the next examples, notice how zeros hold decimal places.

> three thousandths = 0.003   nineteen thousandths = 0.019
> five hundredths = 0.05

Exercise 4

Write each decimal with digits.

1. six hundredths = _____
2. four thousandths = _____
3. twelve thousandths = _____
4. ninety-six thousandths = _____
5. eight thousandths = _____
6. nine hundredths = _____

7. seventeen thousandths = _____
8. three hundredths = _____
9. one hundred six thousandths = _____
10. thirty-two thousandths = _____
11. two hundred two thousandths = _____
12. seventy-eight hundredths = _____

Check your answers on page 193.

Mixed Decimals

A **mixed decimal** has a whole number and a decimal. A decimal point separates the whole number from the decimal. Read "and" where you see the decimal point.

> Read 1.75 as "one and seventy-five hundredths."
> Read 20.6 as "twenty and six tenths."
> Read 3.012 as "three and twelve thousandths."

Exercise 5

For each problem, fill in the blank to complete the name of the decimal.

1. 2.4 = two _____ four _____
2. 3.36 = three _____ thirty-six _____
3. 14.002 = fourteen _____ two _____
4. 20.09 = twenty _____ nine _____
5. 50.8 = fifty _____ eight _____
6. 9.032 = nine _____ thirty-two _____
7. 5.011 = five _____ eleven _____
8. 61.07 = sixty-one _____ seven _____

Check your answers on page 193.

In the next examples, notice how zeros hold decimal places.

> four and two thousandths = 4.002   three and forty-two thousandths = 3.042
> ten and nine hundredths = 10.09

Exercise 6

Write each mixed decimal with digits.

1. eighty and two hundredths = _____
2. four and seven thousandths = _____
3. nineteen and one hundred six thousandths = _____
4. ten and twenty-one hundredths = _____
5. one hundred forty and five tenths = _____
6. seventy and nine hundred three thousandths = _____
7. one and six hundredths = _____
8. five hundred eight and seven thousandths = _____

Check your answers on page 193.

Equivalent Decimals

You can change a decimal without changing its value by adding one or more zeros to the right end of the decimal. The new number is equal to or **equivalent** to the original number.

> **LANGUAGE Tip**
>
> The word root *equal* is found in these words:
>
> equivalent — equal to
>
> equilateral — with equal sides
>
> equalize — make equal
>
> equidistant — equal distance from

> Change 0.4 (four tenths) to thousandths.
> 0.4 = 0.400   Thousandths has three decimal places.
>   Add two zeros to the right of 0.4.
> Change 7.8 (seven and eight tenths) to hundredths.
> 7.8 = 7.80   Hundredths has two decimal places.
>   Add one zero to the right of 7.8.

> **Math Note**
>
> When you add a decimal point and one or more zeros to the right of a whole number, you do not change the value of the original number. For example, $15 = 15.00$.

Exercise 7

Circle the pair of equivalent decimals in each group of numbers.

1. 0.57   0.057   0.570
2. 0.900   0.9   0.09
3. 0.824   0.82400   0.08240
4. 0.031   3.10   3.1

5. 7.45   7.045   7.450
6. 5.00   5   0.500
7. 2000   20   20.00
8. 36.30   36.3   3.63

Change each number to an equivalent number written in hundredths.

9. 0.8 = _____   11. 1.3 = _____   13. 12.6 = _____   15. 9 = _____
10. 0.5 = _____   12. 6.9 = _____   14. 22.2 = _____   16. 25 = _____

Change each number to an equivalent number written in thousandths.

17. 0.32 = _____   19. 0.75 = _____   21. 7.9 = _____   23. 38 = _____
18. 0.7 = _____   20. 2.18 = _____   22. 19.64 = _____   24. 50 = _____

Check your answers on page 194.

Simplifying Decimals

The answers to decimal problems often end with zeros. When the answer to a problem is 1.4500, the calculator shows 1.45 as the answer.

1.45 and 1.4500 are equivalent decimals. The calculator **simplifies** the decimal by dropping the last two zeros. Simplified decimals are often easier to work with.

> Simplify 2.530
>
> $$2.530 = 2.53$$ Drop the zero at the right of 2.53.

> **Math Note**
>
> Zeros at the left of mixed decimals can also be dropped. For example, 03.28 is easier to read when it is written 3.28. When there is no whole number, a zero is often left in the ones place. The decimal .45 can be written as the equivalent decimal 0.45.

Exercise 8

Simplify each number.

1. 0.360 = _____
2. 0.700 = _____
3. 0.0400 = _____

4. 3.00   = _____
5. 5.600   = _____
6. 10.0100 = _____

7. 28.000 = _____
8. 2.5050 = _____
9. 14.100 = _____

Check your answers on page 194.

 ## On Your Calculator

Follow these steps to enter the mixed decimal 5.4 on your calculator.

1. Clear your calculator.

2. Enter the whole number.

3. Press the decimal point key.

4. Enter the decimal.

5. Read the display.

 C 5 .   4   5.4

Comparing Decimals

Sometimes it is difficult to decide which of two decimals is greater. Your problem will be easier to solve if the two numbers have the same number of decimal places. Put zeros to the right of the decimal with fewer decimal places until the numbers have the same number of decimal places. Then compare the decimals.

> Which is greater, 0.2 or 0.15?
>
> 0.2 = 0.20   Since 0.15 has two decimal places, put a zero to the right of 0.2.
>   20 hundredths is more than 15 hundredths.
>   0.2 is greater than 0.15.

Exercise 9

Circle the larger decimal in each pair.

1. 0.4 or 0.35

2. 0.15 or 0.9

3. 0.07 or 0.17

4. 0.56 or 0.572

5. 0.08 or 0.076

6. 0.219 or 0.29

7. 0.66 or 0.7

8. 0.528 or 0.51

9. 0.039 or 0.1

10. 0.81 or 0.808

11. 0.063 or 0.07

12. 0.9 or 0.88

13. 0.443 or 0.004

14. 0.05 or 0.115

15. 0.073 or 0.37

Check your answers on page 194.

 ## On Your Calculator

Follow these steps to enter the decimal 0.18 on your calculator.

1. Clear your calculator.

3. Enter the number.

2. Press the decimal point key.

4. Read the display.

  C . 1 8   0.18

Rounding Decimals

When you add, subtract, multiply, and divide decimals, it is useful to estimate answers. To estimate, you often need to round numbers.

To round to a decimal place, look at the digit to the right.

If the digit to the right is less than 5, round down.

If the digit to the right is 5 or more, round up.

> Round 4.72 to the nearest one.
> Since the digit to the right of the ones is 7, round up. $4.72 \approx 5$.
> Round 2.93 to the nearest tenth.
> Since the digit to the right of the tenths is 3, round down. $2.93 \approx 2.9$.
> Round 0.018 to the nearest hundredth.
> Since the digit to the right of the hundredths is 8, round up. $0.018 \approx 0.02$.

Exercise 10

Round each number to the nearest one.

1. $15.29 \approx$ _____
2. $126.09 \approx$ _____
3. $9.715 \approx$ _____

Round each number to the nearest tenth.

4. $0.513 \approx$ _____
5. $62.88 \approx$ _____
6. $6.439 \approx$ _____

Round each number to the nearest hundredth.

7. $0.043 \approx$ _____
8. $6.259 \approx$ _____
9. $56.908 \approx$ _____

Check your answers on page 194.

Points to Remember

- The first three decimal places (in order from greatest to least value) are tenths, hundredths, and thousandths.

- In a mixed decimal, a decimal point separates the whole number from the decimal.

- To change a decimal to an equivalent decimal, add one or more zeros to the right of the last digit.

- To simplify a decimal, drop zeros at the right end of the decimal.

- To compare decimals, give the decimals the same number of places by adding zeros to the right of the last digit.

Chapter 10

Decimal Checkup

Use the number 2.916 to answer questions 1–3.

1. The digit 9 is in what number place? _____

2. The digit 1 is in what number place? _____

3. The digit 6 is in what number place? _____

Fill in each blank.

4. In the number 12.84, the digit 8 represents 8 of the _____ equal parts of 1.

5. In the number 0.175, the digit 7 represents 7 of the _____ equal parts of 1.

6. In words, 0.061 = sixty-one _____.

Use numbers to write each decimal or mixed decimal.

7. eleven hundredths = _____

8. fifty-three thousandths = _____

9. four tenths = _____

10. nine and seven hundredths = _____

11. seventeen and eight thousandths = _____

Answer each of the following questions.

12. Express 0.25 as an equivalent decimal in thousandths. _____

13. Circle the two numbers that are equivalent. 0.38 0.038 0.380

14. Which number is greater, 0.41 or 0.095? _____

15. Round 0.493 to the nearest tenth. _____

16. Round 18.206 to the nearest hundredth. _____

Check your answers on page 194.

Calculating with Decimals

In real life, we often need to solve problems with decimals. Read these four problems. Decide whether you would add, subtract, multiply, or divide to get each answer. Then explain why you chose that operation.

1. Normal body temperature is 98.6 degrees. Mark's temperature rose to 101 degrees. How much above normal was his temperature?

2. Carla bought 3 packages of ground beef. One package weighed 1.01 pounds, another weighed 0.97 pound, and the third weighed 0.87 pound. How many pounds did she buy altogether?

3. A car traveled 150.8 miles on 6.4 gallons of gasoline. How many miles did the car get per gallon?

4. One yard of silk costs $12.99. If Ann buys 2.75 yards, how much will she pay?

Subtract the numbers in (**1**) because the answer is the *difference*.

Add the numbers in (**2**) because the answer is the *total amount*.

Divide the numbers in (**3**) because you are looking for *equal parts of a total*.

Multiply the numbers in (**4**) because you need to find the total cost when you know how much each yard costs.

In this chapter, you will use basic operations with decimals. You will continue to learn how to solve and check problems.

Adding Decimals

The numbers in addition problems often have a different number of decimal places. To make it easier to add the numbers, change the numbers so they all have the same number of decimal places.

When you write a decimal addition problem, line up the decimal points. Write tenths under tenths, hundredths under hundredths, and so on. Remember to write a decimal point in your answer.

It rained three days last week. On Sunday, it rained 0.5 inch; on Monday, 1 inch; and on Tuesday, 0.75 inch. What was the total rainfall for the week?

```
  1
  0.5 0      The number 0.75 has two decimal places.
  1.0 0      Write a 0 to the right of 0.5 and two 0s to the right of 1.
+ 0.7 5      Add the hundredths: 0 + 0 + 5 = 5.
  2.2 5      Add the tenths: 5 + 0 + 7 = 12.
                Write 2 under the tenths and carry 1 to the ones.
             Add the ones: 1 + 0 + 1 + 0 = 2.
             The total rainfall for the week was 2.25 inches.
```

Exercise 1

Solve each problem. Then check your answers. If any answer is not correct, redo the problem.

1. $0.5 + 0.17 =$

2. $0.099 + 0.45 =$

3. $3.694 + 8.1 =$

4. $4 + 0.759 =$

5. $0.807 + 0.093 =$

6. $14.3 + 1.976 =$

7. $3.8 + 0.562 + 21.4 =$

8. $0.008 + 0.06 + 0.9 =$

9. $7.6 + 9 + 12.09 =$

10. $0.653 + 0.8 + 1.4 =$

11. $0.79 + 1.2 + 16 =$

12. $4.5 + 1.93 + 0.283 =$

Check your answers on page 194.

Subtracting Decimals

When subtracting decimals, line up the decimal points. If the numbers have a different number of decimal places, change the numbers so they all have the same number of decimal places.

If a digit in the top number is smaller than the digit you are subtracting, you need to borrow. Read the next example carefully.

Ellen estimated that she could type a report in 2.25 hours. She finished the report in 1.5 hours. How much sooner did she finish typing the report than she expected?

$$\begin{array}{r} {\scriptstyle 1\ \ 12} \\ 2.\cancel{2}5 \\ -\ 1.50 \\ \hline 0.75 \end{array}$$

Since 2.25 has two decimal places, write a 0 to the right of 1.5.
Subtract the hundredths: $5 - 0 = 5$.
Borrow 1 from the ones. Now there is 1 one.
Add the 1 to the 2 in the tenths column.
$$10 \text{ tenths} + 2 \text{ tenths} = 12 \text{ tenths}$$
Subtract the new tenths: $12 - 5 = 7$.
Subtract the new ones: $1 - 1 = 0$.
Ellen finished 0.75 hour sooner than she expected.

Exercise 2

Rewrite these problems in columns. Be sure the numbers in each problem have the same number of decimal places. Solve the problems, and check your answers.

1. $0.84 - 0.3 \quad =$

2. $0.5 - 0.209 \quad =$

3. $0.77 - 0.614 =$

4. $3.855 - 0.73 =$

5. $4 - 1.16 \quad =$

6. $9.9 - 7.35 \quad =$

7. $10.3 - 2.898 =$

8. $21.57 - 16.4 =$

9. $20 - 15.553 =$

10. $1.2 - 0.865 =$

11. $13 - 11.37 \quad =$

12. $40 - 16.2 \quad =$

Check your answers on page 194.

Multiplying Decimals

When multiplying decimals, you can write the numbers in any order. It is easier if you put the number with fewer digits on the bottom. Multiply the digits as if they were whole numbers. When you have the product, you can determine where the decimal point should go.

Count the total number of decimal places in the problem. Then count off the same number of decimal places in the answer. Begin counting places on the right.

What is the product of 8.2 × 7?

```
  1
 8.2     1 decimal place
× 7      0 decimal places
57.4     1 decimal place
```

Rewrite the problem with 8.2 on top.
Multiply 7 × 2 = 14; write 4 and carry 1.
Multiply 7 × 8 = 56, and add 1: 56 + 1 = 57.
There is a total of only 1 decimal place.
The product is 57.4.

Find the product of 0.5 and 3.6.

```
   3
  3.6     1 decimal place
× 0.5     1 decimal place
 1.8 0    2 decimal places
```

Rewrite the problem with 3.6 on top.
Multiply 5 × 6 = 30; write 0 and carry 3.
Multiply 5 × 3 = 15, and add 3: 15 + 3 = 18.
There is a total of 2 decimal places.
The product is 1.80, which simplifies to 1.8.

Exercise 3

Solve each problem. You can check your answers on a calculator. If any answer is not correct, redo the problem.

1. 9.5 × 8   =
2. 6 × 0.46   =
3. 7.8 × 0.3   =
4. 0.29 × 0.7 =

5. 0.4 × 6.03 =
6. 20.8 × 0.6 =
7. 0.313 × 4 =
8. 0.2 × 0.97 =

9. 0.43 × 0.8 =
10. 1.05 × 0.9 =
11. 6 × 0.15   =
12. 0.3 × 4.7   =

Check your answers on page 194.

Thinking About Answers

When you multiply any number by a whole number greater than 1, the answer will be greater than the other number in the problem. For example, the answer to 2×0.6 will be greater than 0.6.

Exercise 4

Solve each problem. The answer to each problem should be larger than the decimal or the mixed decimal in the problem. Use a calculator to check your work.

1. $2 \times 3.15 =$ 3. $5 \times 0.65 =$ 5. $7.025 \times 6 =$ 7. $9 \times 8.6 \quad =$

2. $6.1 \times 3 \quad =$ 4. $4 \times 4.74 =$ 6. $10.9 \times 8 \quad =$ 8. $0.29 \times 40 =$

Check your answers on page 194.

When you multiply any number by a decimal, the answer will be *part of* the other number. In other words, the answer will be less than the other number in the problem.

What is 4.5×0.8?		
4		Rewrite the problem with 4.5 on top.
4.5	I decimal place	Multiply $8 \times 5 = 40$; write 0 and carry 4.
$\times$ 0.8	I decimal place	Multiply $8 \times 4 = 32$, and add 4: $32 + 4 = 36$.
3.6 0	2 decimal places	There is a total of 2 decimal places.
		The product is 3.60, which simplifies to 3.6.
		Notice that the answer, 3.6, is less than 4.5.

Exercise 5

Solve each problem. The answer to each of these problems should be less than the whole number or mixed decimal in the problem. Use a calculator to check your work.

1. $0.3 \times 15 \quad =$ 3. $2.6 \times 0.8 \quad =$ 5. $1.5 \times 0.7 \quad =$ 7. $0.1 \times 14 \quad =$

2. $0.2 \times 28 \quad =$ 4. $1.07 \times 0.5 =$ 6. $0.9 \times 4.3 \quad =$ 8. $0.4 \times 5.08 =$

Check your answers on page 194.

Two-Digit Multipliers

When you multiply by a two-digit number, you must do several steps. (For a review, reread pages 51–52.) Once you find the final product, decide where the decimal point should go. Count the number of decimal places in the problem. Then put the same number of decimal places in the answer.

A suitcase cost $69. A store put the suitcase on sale for 0.75 of the regular price. What is the sale price?

$$
\begin{array}{r}
\$ 6\,9 \\
\times\ 0.7\,5 \\
\hline
3\,4\,5 \\
4\,8\,3 \\
\hline
\$5\,1.7\,5
\end{array}
$$

Multiply $5 \times 9 = 45$. Write 5 and carry 4.
Multiply $5 \times 6 = 30$, and add 4. $30 + 4 = 34$.
    The first partial product is 345.
Multiply $7 \times 9 = 63$. Write 3 and carry 6.
Multiply $7 \times 6 = 42$, and add 6. $42 + 6 = 48$.
    The second partial product is 483.
Add the partial products.
The problem has 2 decimal places.
Put 2 decimal places in the answer.
The sale price of the suitcase is $51.75.

Exercise 6

Solve each problem, and check your answers. Redo incorrect problems.

1. $0.33 \times 7.6 =$
4. $2.8 \times 34.9 =$
7. $1.4 \times 5.21 =$

2. $3.1 \times 5.8 =$
5. $67 \times 2.08 =$
8. $0.45 \times 72 =$

3. $0.75 \times 2.9 =$
6. $0.18 \times 12.7 =$
9. $0.63 \times 8.4 =$

Check your answers on page 194.

Multiplying by 10, 100, and 1,000

Multiplication problems with two-digit multipliers are not always as complicated as the problems in the last three exercises.

Multiply 6.7×10.

6.7	Multiply $0 \times 7 = 0$ and write 0.
$\times\,1\,0$	Multiply $0 \times 6 = 0$ and write 0.
$0\,0$	Multiply $1 \times 7 = 7$ and write 7.
$6\,7$	Multiply $1 \times 6 = 6$ and write 6.
$6\,7.0$	The product is 67.0, which simplifies to 67.

Notice that in the answer to the problem, the decimal point in 6.7 moved one place to the right. Multiplying by 100 and multiplying by 1,000 are also easy operations.

Math Note

- To multiply by 10, move the decimal point one place to the right.
- To multiply by 100, move the decimal point two places to the right.
- To multiply by 1,000, move the decimal point three places to the right.

Look at these examples.

$10 \times 0.48 = 4.8$	Move the decimal point in 0.48 one place to the right.
$100 \times 12.6 = 1,260.$	To move the decimal point two places, add one 0.
$1,000 \times 7.2 = 7,200.$	To move the decimal point three places, add two 0s.

Exercise 7

Write the answer to each problem. Check your answers on a calculator. Redo any problem that was not correct.

1. $2.6 \times 10 \quad =$ _____
2. $0.129 \times 10 =$ _____
3. $10 \times 4.03 \quad =$ _____
4. $0.77 \times 10 \quad =$ _____

5. $100 \times 8.6 \quad =$ _____
6. $51.2 \times 100 \quad =$ _____
7. $100 \times 0.044 =$ _____
8. $7.09 \times 100 \quad =$ _____

9. $4.6 \times 1,000 \quad =$ _____
10. $0.088 \times 1,000 =$ _____
11. $1,000 \times 0.65 \quad =$ _____
12. $0.002 \times 1,000 =$ _____

Check your answers on page 194.

Dividing Decimals by Whole Numbers

To divide decimals by whole numbers, follow the same steps you used for dividing whole numbers. (Review dividing on pages 61–68.) Place the decimal point in your answer directly above the decimal point in the problem before you start dividing.

Sometimes one number does not divide evenly into another number. To continue dividing, you may need to add one or more zeros at the end of the dividend.

Sam is planning an 8.5-mile hike. He wants to do the hike in 3 equal parts. To the nearest tenth, how many miles will there be between stops?

```
    2.8 3
 3 )8.5 0
   - 6
     2 5
   - 2 4
       1 0
      - 9
         1
```

First: Bring up the decimal point.

Then: Divide $8 \div 3 = 2$ with a remainder.
Multiply $2 \times 3 = 6$, and subtract $8 - 6 = 2$.
Bring down the next digit, 5.

Then: Divide $25 \div 3 = 8$ with a remainder.
Multiply $8 \times 3 = 24$, and subtract $25 - 24 = 1$.
Write a 0 to the right of 5, and bring it down.

Then: Divide $10 \div 3 = 3$ with a remainder.
Multiply $3 \times 3 = 9$, and subtract $10 - 9 = 1$.
Round 2.83 to the nearest tenth. $2.83 \approx 2.8$ miles

Think about the last example. You can continue to write zeros, but you will never get an even answer. The answer will be 2.833… with the digit 3 continuing to repeat. A decimal like this is called a **repeating decimal**. You can round answers like this to a certain place, such as tenths or hundredths.

Exercise 8

Solve each problem. Round answers that do not divide evenly to the nearest hundredth. Check your answers. If any answer is not correct, redo the problem.

1. $4.4 \div 8 =$
2. $0.65 \div 5 =$
3. $6.8 \div 4 =$
4. $13.9 \div 6 =$
5. $2.66 \div 7 =$
6. $20.3 \div 9 =$
7. $7.8 \div 12 =$
8. $0.9 \div 15 =$
9. $7.2 \div 20 =$
10. $3.6 \div 7 =$
11. $75.3 \div 30 =$
12. $5.26 \div 16 =$

Check your answers on page 194.

Writing Equivalent Problems

To divide by a decimal, change the problem to an equivalent problem with a whole number as the divisor. Move the decimal point in the divisor to make the divisor a whole number. Then move the decimal point in the dividend the same number of places. Moving the decimal points in this way is like multiplying both numbers by 10, 100, or 1,000. You may need to add zeros to the right end of the dividend.

Place the decimal point in your answer directly above the new decimal point.

Change $0.8 \overline{)7.2}$ to an equivalent problem with a whole number divisor.

$0.8 \overline{)7.2} = 8. \overline{)72.}$ First move the decimal point in 0.8 one place to the right. Then move the decimal point in 7.2 one place to the right. (This is like multiplying both numbers by 10.)

Change $0.15 \overline{)0.675}$ to an equivalent problem with a whole number divisor.

$0.15 \overline{)0.675} = 15. \overline{)67.5}$ First move the point in 0.15 two places to the right. Then move the point in 0.675 two places to the right. (This is like multiplying both numbers by 100.)

Change $0.009 \overline{)2.7}$ to an equivalent problem with a whole number divisor.

$0.009 \overline{)2.7} = 9. \overline{)2,700.}$ First move the point in 0.009 three places to the right. Then move the point in 2.7 three places to the right. (This is like multiplying both numbers by 1,000.)

Exercise 9

Rewrite each problem with a whole number divisor. First move the decimal point in the divisor. Then move the decimal point in the dividend the same number of places. Do not solve the problems.

1. $0.12 \overline{)2.76}$

2. $0.3 \overline{)3.75}$

3. $0.008 \overline{)5.92}$

4. $0.7 \overline{)0.252}$

5. $1.6 \overline{)7.2}$

6. $0.032 \overline{)7.68}$

Check your answers on page 195.

Dividing by Decimals

Once you have moved the decimal point in both the divisor and the dividend, you are ready to solve the problem.

> At her temporary job, Linda received $81.75 for 7.5 hours of work. How much did she make per hour?
>
> $$7.5\,\overline{)\$81.75} = 75.\,\overline{)\$8\,1\,7.5\,0}$$
>
> ```
>         $ 1 0.9 0
> 75. )$8 1 7.5 0
>     - 7 5
>       6 7
>      -  0
>       6 7 5
>     - 6 7 5
>         0 0
> ```
>
> First move the point in 7.5 one place to the right.
> Then move the point in $81.75 one place to the right.
> (This is like multiplying both numbers by 10.)
> Place the point in the answer above the new point.
> Divide.
> Linda makes $10.90 per hour.

When you use a calculator to solve division problems, you do not need to move the decimal points in either the divisor or the dividend.

Exercise 10

Rewrite and solve each problem. Round any answer that does not come out evenly to the nearest hundredth. You can check your answers on a calculator.

1. $5.4 \div 0.2 \ =$
2. $96 \div 0.8 \ =$
3. $0.125 \div 0.5 =$
4. $0.963 \div 0.3 =$

5. $20 \div 0.6 \ =$
6. $45 \div 0.09 =$
7. $2.8 \div 0.16 =$
8. $0.64 \div 1.8 =$

9. $3 \div 0.075 \ =$
10. $0.576 \div 0.048 =$
11. $0.792 \div 0.33 \ =$
12. $1.3 \div 0.15 \ =$

Check your answers on page 195.

For more practice, solve the problems in Exercise 9 and check your answers on a calculator.

Dividing by 10, 100, and 1,000

Earlier in this chapter you learned shortcuts for multiplying by 10, 100, and 1,000. Dividing by 10, dividing by 100, and dividing by 1,000 are also easy operations.

Find the quotient of $4.9 \div 10$.

$$\begin{array}{r} 0.4\,9 \\ 1\,0\,\overline{)4.9\,0} \\ -\,4\,0 \\ \hline 9\,0 \\ -\,9\,0 \\ \hline 0 \end{array}$$

First: Bring up the decimal point.

Then: Divide $49 \div 10 = 4$ with a remainder.
Multiply $4 \times 10 = 40$, and subtract $49 - 40 = 9$.
Write a 0 to the right of 9, and bring it down.

Then: Divide $90 \div 10 = 9$.
Multiply $9 \times 10 = 90$, and subtract $90 - 90 = 0$.

Notice that in the answer to the problem, the decimal point in 4.9 moves one place to the left.

Math Note

- To divide a number by 10, move the decimal point one place to the left.

- To divide a number by 100, move the decimal point two places to the left.

- To divide a number by 1,000, move the decimal point three places to the left.

Look at these examples.

$2.8 \div 10 = 0.28$ Move the point in 2.8 one place to the left.

$0.4 \div 100 = 0.004$ Write another zero and move the point in 0.4 two places left.

$673 \div 1,000 = 0.673$ Move the point in 673 three places to the left.
(The number 673 is understood to have a point at the right.)

Exercise 11

Write the answer to each problem. Check your answers on a calculator. Redo any problem that was not correct.

1. $5.2 \div 10 =$ _____

2. $47 \div 10 =$ _____

3. $12.5 \div 10 =$ _____

4. $\$42 \div 10 =$ _____

5. $29.3 \div 100 =$ _____

6. $8.7 \div 100 =$ _____

7. $0.6 \div 100 =$ _____

8. $\$23 \div 100 =$ _____

9. $405 \div 1,000 =$ _____

10. $71 \div 1,000 =$ _____

11. $8,569 \div 1,000 =$ _____

12. $\$60 \div 1,000 =$ _____

Check your answers on page 195.

Decimal Word Problems

One way to estimate answers to decimal problems is to round each mixed decimal to the nearest whole number. Then do the math.

> What is the combined weight of a package that weighs 3.5 pounds and another package that weighs 14.6 pounds?
>
> $$3.5 \approx 4$$
> $$+ \ 14.6 \approx + \ 15$$
> exact answer → 18.1 pounds   19 pounds ← estimate

Strategy: A Problem-Solving Strategy

- State the problem in your own words.
- List the facts.
- Choose the mathematical operation.
- Estimate so you know what a reasonable answer will be.
- Solve for the exact answer.

Exercise 12

For each problem, first estimate an answer. Then find the exact answer.

1. A recipe calls for a 3.5-pound chicken. Sandra bought a 2.74-pound chicken. How much less does she have than the recipe calls for?

    Estimate   Exact

2. A recipe calls for 8 ounces of tomato paste. The store sells only 3.125-ounce cans. How many ounces of tomato paste are there in two cans?

    Estimate   Exact

3. A can of juice contains 24.3 fluid ounces. The label says there are 6 servings in a can. How many ounces are in each serving?

    Estimate   Exact

4. A cheese shop is having a sale. Phil bought 1.79 pounds of Monterey Jack and 2 pounds of cheddar. How many pounds of cheese did he buy altogether?

    Estimate   Exact

5. The trip odometer in Jed's car has a reading of 314.9 miles. If Jed has been driving for 5 hours, about how far did he drive each hour? Find the answer to the nearest mile.

Estimate	Exact

LANGUAGE Tip

Context Clue

The word *odometer* is used in question 5. The problem says that the odometer is in a car. It also says that the odometer is read in "miles." An odometer measures the miles you have driven.

6. A box of cereal weighs 1.32 pounds. What is the total weight of a shipment of 100 boxes of cereal?

Estimate	Exact

7. There are 1.6 kilometers in 1 mile. Find the distance in kilometers between two cities that are 65 miles apart.

Estimate	Exact

8. Normal body temperature is 98.6 degrees. When Malcolm had a fever, his temperature rose 5.8 degrees. What was his temperature when he had a fever?

Estimate	Exact

9. The average rainfall in November in San Juan, Puerto Rico, is 5.9 inches. Last year the rainfall in November was 1.55 inches more than the average. How much rain fell in San Juan last November?

Estimate	Exact

10. Jackie drove 153 miles in 2.5 hours. What average distance did she drive in one hour?

Estimate	Exact

Check your answers on page 195.

Points to Remember

- When adding and subtracting decimals, give all the numbers the same number of decimal places. Adding zeros to the right of a decimal does not change the value of the decimal. For example, $0.7 = 0.700$.

- When multiplying decimals, count the number of decimal places in the problem. Put that total number of decimal places in the answer.

- When dividing by a decimal, move the decimal point so the divisor is a whole number. Then move the decimal point in the dividend the same number of places.

Decimal Checkup

1. $4.57 + 16 + 9.043 =$

2. $0.73 + 0.158 + 0.6 =$

3. $6 - 2.387$ =

4. $30.7 - 18.95$ =

5. 3.5×12.5 =

6. 0.8×3.26 =

7. $10 \times 0.738 =$

8. $4.09 \times 100 =$

9. $3.24 \div 9$ =

10. $5.74 \div 2.8 =$

11. $36.7 \div 100 =$

12. $50 \div 1,000 =$

For each problem, first estimate an answer. Then find the exact answer.

13. An airplane flew at an average speed of 390 miles per hour for 2.1 hours. How far did the plane fly?

Estimate	Exact

14. From a board 3.6 meters long, Nick cut a piece 1.35 meters long. Find the length of the remaining piece.

Estimate	Exact

15. What is the total weight of 6.8 pounds of meat, 4.35 pounds of cheese, and 2 pounds of flour?

Estimate	Exact

16. Annabel paid $75.40 for 4.5 yards of material. What was the cost of one yard?

Estimate	Exact

Check your answers on page 195.

UNIT 4

Fractions

In this unit, you will learn the basic skills needed for working with fractions. You will learn how to

- describe the parts of a fraction

- express amounts with fractions and mixed numbers

- compare fractions

- write equivalent (equal) fractions

- add, subtract, multiply, and divide fractions

- estimate answers

Chapter 12

Fractions Basics

In Units 2 and 3, you learned about decimals. Decimals describe equal parts of a whole. With decimals, one whole is divided into tenths, hundredths, thousandths, and so on.

Fractions are another way of describing parts of a whole. When one whole is divided into two equal parts, each part is $\frac{1}{2}$ (one-half) of the whole.

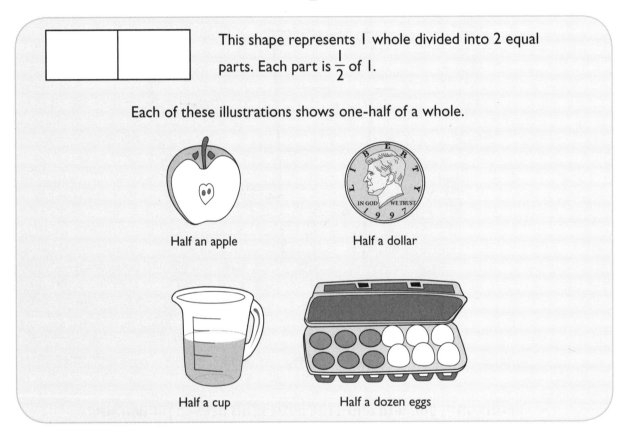

This shape represents 1 whole divided into 2 equal parts. Each part is $\frac{1}{2}$ of 1.

Each of these illustrations shows one-half of a whole.

Half an apple

Half a dollar

Half a cup

Half a dozen eggs

In this chapter, you will learn to express amounts as fractions. You will also learn to compare fractions and to round them to whole numbers.

Talk Math

Do these activities with a partner or a group.

1. Describe situations in which you use fractions.
2. With a partner, take turns giving an example of half of 1 whole and saying what the whole is. For example, you might say, "Half an hour." Your partner should say, "The whole is one hour."

Equal Parts of One

Get a sheet of paper. The paper represents 1 whole. Fold the paper in half. (See Figure A.) Now unfold the paper. How many equal parts do you see?

The sheet of paper is divided into two equal parts, or two **halves** $\left(\frac{2}{2}\right)$. Each equal part is one-half $\left(\frac{1}{2}\right)$.

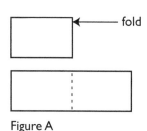

Figure A

Refold the paper. Then fold it in half again. (See Figure B.) Unfold the paper. How many equal parts are there?

The sheet of paper is divided into 4 equal parts, or four **fourths** $\left(\frac{4}{4}\right)$. Each equal part is one-fourth $\left(\frac{1}{4}\right)$.

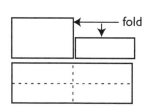

Figure B

Refold the paper again. Then fold it one more time. (See Figure C.) Unfold the paper. How many equal parts are there now?

The sheet is divided into 8 equal parts, or eight **eighths** $\left(\frac{8}{8}\right)$. Each part is one-eighth $\left(\frac{1}{8}\right)$.

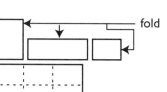

Figure C

Exercise 1

1. The triangle is divided into how many equal parts? _____

2. Each part is what fraction of the triangle? _____

3. The rectangle is divided into how many equal parts? _____

4. Each part is what fraction of the rectangle? _____

5. The circle is divided into how many equal parts? _____

6. Each part is what fraction of the circle? _____

Check your answers on page 195.

Naming Equal Parts

A fraction is written with two whole numbers separated by a line. The **numerator** at the top tells the number of equal parts being discussed. The **denominator** at the bottom tells the number of equal parts in 1 whole.

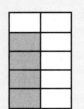

What fraction of the figure is shaded?

The figure is divided into 10 equal parts.

4 parts are shaded. $\frac{4}{10}$ of the figure is shaded.

What fraction of the figure is *not* shaded?

6 parts of the figure are not shaded.

$\frac{6}{10}$ of the figure is not shaded.

To read a fraction, first say the numerator, and then say the denominator. Read the fractions in the example as "4 tenths" and "6 tenths."

How would you write 1 whole as a fraction? If the whole is divided into 10 equal parts, $\frac{10}{10}$ equals the whole. You could also write 1 whole as $\frac{1}{1}, \frac{2}{2}, \frac{3}{3}$, and so on.

Exercise 2

Each shape represents 1 whole. For each fraction, write the fraction that names the whole, the shaded portion, and the unshaded portion.

1. a. 1 whole: _____
    b. shaded portion: _____
    c. unshaded portion: _____

2. a. 1 whole: _____
    b. shaded portion: _____
    c. unshaded portion: _____

3. a. 1 whole: _____
    b. shaded portion: _____
    c. unshaded portion: _____

4. a. 1 whole: _____
    b. shaded portion: _____
    c. unshaded portion: _____

Check your answers on page 195.

Comparing Fractions with Numerators of 1

LANGUAGE Tip

Here is a clue to help you remember which number is the denominator:

The **down** number is the **denominator**.

The denominator of a fraction tells how many parts the whole is divided into. When the denominator is small, the whole is divided into only a few equal parts. When the denominator is large, the whole is divided into many equal parts.

The fraction table below shows 7 rectangles, each representing 1 whole. The rectangles are divided into halves, thirds, fourths, fifths, sixths, eighths, and tenths.

Think about the size of the fractional parts. When 1 whole is divided into fewer parts, each part is larger.

$1 =$	$\frac{1}{2}$					$\frac{1}{2}$					$= \frac{2}{2}$
$1 =$	$\frac{1}{3}$			$\frac{1}{3}$			$\frac{1}{3}$				$= \frac{3}{3}$
$1 =$	$\frac{1}{4}$		$\frac{1}{4}$		$\frac{1}{4}$			$\frac{1}{4}$			$= \frac{4}{4}$
$1 =$	$\frac{1}{5}$		$\frac{1}{5}$		$\frac{1}{5}$		$\frac{1}{5}$		$\frac{1}{5}$		$= \frac{5}{5}$
$1 =$	$\frac{1}{6}$		$\frac{1}{6}$	$\frac{1}{6}$		$\frac{1}{6}$		$\frac{1}{6}$		$\frac{1}{6}$	$= \frac{6}{6}$
$1 =$	$\frac{1}{8}$	$\frac{1}{8}$	$\frac{1}{8}$	$\frac{1}{8}$		$\frac{1}{8}$	$\frac{1}{8}$	$\frac{1}{8}$		$\frac{1}{8}$	$= \frac{8}{8}$
$1 =$	$\frac{1}{10}$	$\frac{1}{10}$	$\frac{1}{10}$	$\frac{1}{10}$	$\frac{1}{10}$	$\frac{1}{10}$	$\frac{1}{10}$	$\frac{1}{10}$	$\frac{1}{10}$	$\frac{1}{10}$	$= \frac{10}{10}$

Which fraction has the greater value: $\frac{1}{2}$ or $\frac{1}{10}$?

As you can see in the table, $\frac{1}{2}$ is greater than $\frac{1}{10}$. Halves are larger parts than tenths.

Exercise 3

Tell which fraction in each pair has the greater value.

1. $\frac{1}{3}$ or $\frac{1}{4}$ _____

2. $\frac{1}{2}$ or $\frac{1}{4}$ _____

3. $\frac{1}{8}$ or $\frac{1}{3}$ _____

4. $\frac{1}{5}$ or $\frac{1}{2}$ _____

5. $\frac{1}{10}$ or $\frac{1}{8}$ _____

6. $\frac{1}{3}$ or $\frac{1}{9}$ _____

7. $\frac{1}{12}$ or $\frac{1}{6}$ _____

8. $\frac{1}{9}$ or $\frac{1}{12}$ _____

9. $\frac{1}{10}$ or $\frac{1}{20}$ _____

Check your answers on page 195.

Comparing Fractions with the Same Numerators or the Same Denominators

When comparing fractions with the same numerators but different denominators, the fraction with the smaller denominator is greater.

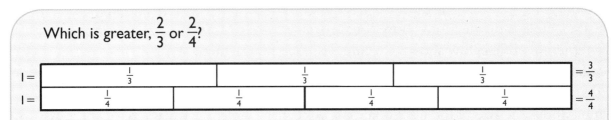

Which is greater, $\frac{2}{3}$ or $\frac{2}{4}$?

Two parts of a whole that is divided into 3 parts are greater than 2 parts of a whole that is divided into 4 parts. $\frac{2}{3}$ is greater than $\frac{2}{4}$ because thirds are larger than fourths.

When comparing fractions with the same denominators but different numerators, the fraction with the larger numerator has the greater value.

Which is greater: $\frac{3}{8}$ or $\frac{5}{8}$?

Both denominators are 8, so the whole has been divided into the same number of parts. Five parts is more than three parts, so $\frac{5}{8}$ is greater than $\frac{3}{8}$.

Exercise 4

Read each sentence. Then choose the fraction that shows the larger amount.

1. A bread recipe calls for $\frac{1}{4}$ cup of wheat bran and $\frac{3}{4}$ cup of oat flour. _____

2. In one class, $\frac{2}{3}$ of the students were men. In another class, $\frac{2}{5}$ were men. _____

3. Typing makes up $\frac{3}{5}$ of Bob's job. Editing makes up $\frac{1}{5}$ of his job. _____

4. At a hardware store, you can buy $\frac{3}{8}$-inch nails or $\frac{3}{4}$-inch nails. _____

5. Aaron's commute takes $\frac{1}{2}$ hour by bus or $\frac{1}{3}$ hour by subway. _____

6. One piece of wood measures $\frac{7}{12}$ foot. A second piece measures $\frac{3}{12}$ foot. _____

Check your answers on page 195.

Improper Fractions

When the numerator of a fraction is equal to or larger than the denominator, the fraction is called an **improper fraction**.

Improper fractions such as $\frac{2}{2}$ and $\frac{8}{4}$ are equal to whole numbers.

$\frac{6}{6}$ = I tin of muffins $\frac{12}{6}$ = 2 tins of muffins

$\underline{12}$ ← number of equal parts being discussed

6 ← total equal parts that I is divided into

Exercise 5

Write an improper fraction that describes each whole amount.

1. _____   2. _____   3. _____

Check your answers on page 195.

Improper fractions such as $\frac{4}{3}$ or $\frac{6}{4}$ represent mixed amounts—a whole plus a fraction.

$\frac{6}{6}$ = I full tin of muffins **and** $\frac{3}{6}$ = the partly filled tin

$\frac{9}{6} = \frac{6}{6} + \frac{3}{6}$

$\underline{9}$ ← number of equal parts being discussed

6 ← total equal parts that I is divided into

Exercise 6

Write an improper fraction that describes each portion.

1. _____   2. _____   3. _____

Check your answers on page 195.

Mixed Numbers

On the last page, you wrote improper fractions to express amounts that are equal to 1 whole or greater than 1 whole. Another way to express these amounts is with mixed numbers. A **mixed number** is a whole number and a fraction.

Write the improper fraction $\frac{3}{2}$ as a mixed number.

$$\frac{3}{2} = \frac{2}{2} + \frac{1}{2} = 1\frac{1}{2}$$

Read the mixed number as, "One and one-half."

Exercise 7

Write a mixed number to describe each point indicated on the scales.

1. a. _____   b. _____   c. _____

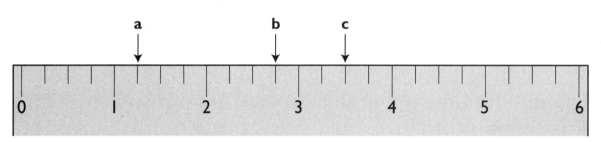

2. a. _____   b. _____   c. _____   d. _____

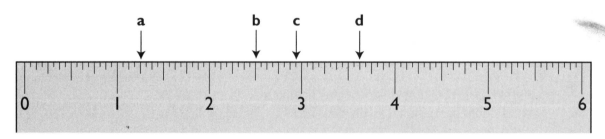

Use digits to write the mixed number mentioned in each sentence.

3. Driving from San Juan to Whitney takes one and one-third hours. _____

4. Apples weighing four and three-fourths pounds cost $10.99. _____

5. In six months, a child grew three and five-sixteenths inches. _____

6. Alex needs three boards, each three and seven-twelfths feet long. _____

7. The freeway sign shows six and one-half miles to the next exit. _____

Check your answers on page 196.

Comparing Fractions to $\frac{1}{2}$

To estimate answers, it helps to know if a fraction is more than $\frac{1}{2}$ or less than $\frac{1}{2}$. A fraction is equal to $\frac{1}{2}$ if the numerator is exactly half of the denominator.

> Write a fraction that is equal to $\frac{1}{2}$ and has a denominator of 6.
>
> Half of 6 is 3. $\qquad\qquad \frac{3}{6} = \frac{1}{2}$

A fraction is less than $\frac{1}{2}$ if the numerator is less than half the denominator.

> Is $\frac{3}{8}$ more or less than $\frac{1}{2}$? The denominator is 8. Half of 8 is 4.
>
> Since the numerator is less than 4, the fraction is less than $\frac{1}{2}$.

A fraction is more than $\frac{1}{2}$ if the numerator is more than half the denominator.

> Is $\frac{7}{12}$ more or less than $\frac{1}{2}$? The denominator is 12. Half of 12 is 6.
>
> Since the numerator is greater than 6, the fraction is more than $\frac{1}{2}$.

Exercise 8

1. Write a fraction that is equal to $\frac{1}{2}$ and has a denominator of 16. _____

2. Is $\frac{13}{20}$ more or less than $\frac{1}{2}$? _____

3. Write a fraction that is equal to $\frac{1}{2}$ and has a denominator of 18. _____

4. Is $\frac{5}{12}$ more or less than $\frac{1}{2}$? _____

5. Write a fraction that is equal to $\frac{1}{2}$ and has a denominator of 24. _____

6. Is $\frac{5}{9}$ more or less than $\frac{1}{2}$? _____

7. Is $\frac{7}{15}$ more or less than $\frac{1}{2}$? _____

Check your answers on page 196.

Rounding to the Nearest Whole Number

When you estimate the answers to fraction problems, it is useful to round mixed numbers to the nearest whole number. Here is one way to round mixed numbers.

If the fraction is less than $\frac{1}{2}$, round the whole number down.

If the fraction is $\frac{1}{2}$ or more, round the whole number up.

Round $2\frac{1}{3}$ to the nearest whole number.

Since $\frac{1}{3}$ is less than $\frac{1}{2}$, round down. $2\frac{1}{3} \approx 2$

Round $3\frac{5}{6}$ to the nearest whole number.

Since $\frac{5}{6}$ is greater than $\frac{1}{2}$, round up. $3\frac{5}{6} \approx 4$

Exercise 9

Round each mixed number to the nearest whole number.

1. $1\frac{1}{4} \approx$ _____
2. $2\frac{3}{5} \approx$ _____
3. $3\frac{2}{5} \approx$ _____
4. $2\frac{1}{6} \approx$ _____

5. $4\frac{3}{8} \approx$ _____
6. $5\frac{2}{3} \approx$ _____
7. $5\frac{4}{5} \approx$ _____
8. $7\frac{3}{16} \approx$ _____

9. $10\frac{1}{2} \approx$ _____
10. $15\frac{3}{4} \approx$ _____
11. $20\frac{3}{10} \approx$ _____
12. $24\frac{7}{8} \approx$ _____

Check your answers on page 196.

Points to Remember

• A fraction represents a part of 1 whole.

• Fractions are written this way: $\frac{numerator}{denominator}$

• When the numerator is equal to or greater than the denominator, the fraction is an improper fraction.

• A mixed number is a whole number plus a fraction.

Fraction Checkup

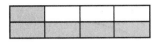

1. What fraction of the rectangle is shaded? _____

2. What fraction of the circle is shaded? _____

3. What fraction of this circle is shaded? _____

4. Write the fraction or mixed number that describes the points marked on the scale.

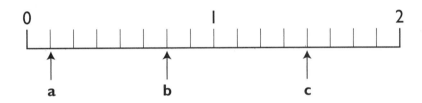

a. _____   b. _____   c. _____

5. Write a fraction equal to $\frac{1}{2}$ with a denominator of 28. _____

Circle the fraction in each pair that has the *smaller* value.

6. $\frac{1}{4}$ or $\frac{3}{4}$ 7. $\frac{2}{5}$ or $\frac{3}{5}$ 8. $\frac{1}{2}$ or $\frac{1}{3}$ 9. $\frac{3}{8}$ or $\frac{5}{8}$

Use digits to write the mixed number mentioned in each sentence.

10. In two days, Al worked a total of six and one-half hours overtime. _____

11. Five large apples weigh two and three-fourths pounds. _____

Round each mixed number to the nearest whole number.

12. $6\frac{5}{8} \approx$ _____

13. $10\frac{3}{16} \approx$ _____

14. $8\frac{1}{2} \approx$ _____

Check your answers on page 196.

Chapter 13

Equivalent Fractions

> **LANGUAGE** *Tip*
>
> *Fraction* and *fracture* (a broken bone) come from the same word root. Both words refer to something that is **broken**.

Equivalent fractions have the same value. Look at some equivalent fractions. Get a sheet of paper.

Fold the paper in half. Then unfold it. Color the left half so you can clearly see $\frac{1}{2}$ of the paper. (See Figure A.)

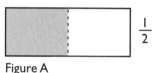

Figure A

Now refold the paper, and then fold it in half again. Unfold the paper. Each folded section is $\frac{1}{4}$. How many fourths equal $\frac{1}{2}$? (See Figure B.) The fractions $\frac{2}{4}$ and $\frac{1}{2}$ represent the same amount. These fractions are equivalent.

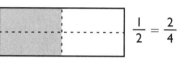

Figure B

Now refold the paper, and then fold it in half one more time. Unfold the paper. Each section is $\frac{1}{8}$. How many eighths equal $\frac{1}{2}$? (See Figure C.) The fraction $\frac{4}{8}$ represents the same amount as $\frac{1}{2}$ and $\frac{2}{4}$. Therefore, $\frac{4}{8}$, $\frac{1}{2}$, and $\frac{2}{4}$ are all equivalent fractions.

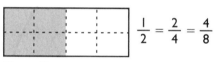

Figure C

In this chapter, you will learn to write equivalent fractions, mixed numbers, and improper fractions. You will also learn to change fractions to decimals and to change decimals to fractions.

Talk Math

Do these activities with a partner or a group.

1. Using your folded sheet of paper, show that $\frac{2}{8} = \frac{1}{4}$ and that $\frac{6}{8} = \frac{3}{4}$.

2. Refold the paper that was folded into eighths. Now fold it in half again.

   How many equal parts is 1 divided into? What fractions are equivalent to $\frac{1}{2}$, $\frac{1}{4}$, and $\frac{3}{4}$?

Writing Equivalent Fractions

Each of these two large rectangles represents 1 whole. The same amount of each rectangle is shaded. In one rectangle, 3 out of 6 parts are shaded. In the other rectangle, 1 out of 2 parts is shaded.

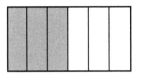

The fractions $\frac{3}{6}$ and $\frac{1}{2}$ represent the same amount. They are **equivalent fractions**.

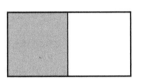

To write an equivalent fraction, multiply both the numerator and the denominator by the same number.

Write fractions equivalent to $\frac{1}{2}$. First multiply by 2, then by 3, and finally by 4.

$$\frac{1 \times 2}{2 \times 2} = \frac{2}{4} \qquad \frac{1 \times 3}{2 \times 3} = \frac{3}{6} \qquad \frac{1 \times 4}{2 \times 4} = \frac{4}{8}$$

$$\frac{1}{2} = \frac{2}{4} \qquad\qquad \frac{1}{2} = \frac{3}{6} \qquad\qquad \frac{1}{2} = \frac{4}{8}$$

When you add and subtract fractions, you will need to write equivalent fractions with larger denominators. First divide the new denominator by the old denominator. Then multiply the old numerator by the quotient.

Change $\frac{2}{3}$ to an equivalent fraction with a denominator of 12.

$12 \div 3 = 4$ First, divide the denominators.
The new denominator is 4 times the old denominator.

$\frac{2 \times 4}{3 \times 4} = \frac{8}{12}$ Multiply both the numerator and the denominator by 4.

$$\frac{2}{3} = \frac{8}{12}$$

Exercise 1

1. $\frac{1}{2} = \frac{}{6}$ 3. $\frac{3}{4} = \frac{}{8}$ 5. $\frac{2}{5} = \frac{}{15}$ 7. $\frac{3}{8} = \frac{}{24}$

2. $\frac{1}{3} = \frac{}{6}$ 4. $\frac{2}{5} = \frac{}{10}$ 6. $\frac{5}{6} = \frac{}{12}$ 8. $\frac{2}{3} = \frac{}{9}$

Check your answers on page 196.

Finding a Common Denominator

To add or subtract fractions, the denominators must be alike. If the denominators are different, change the fractions to equivalent fractions with the same denominators.

A number that every denominator in a problem can divide into evenly is called a **common denominator**. The *smallest* number that all the denominators in a problem can divide into evenly is called the **lowest common denominator.**

Here are three ways to find the lowest common denominator.

(1) If one denominator can be divided evenly by the other denominator(s), then that is the common denominator.

> Find the lowest common denominator for $\frac{1}{8}$ and $\frac{1}{2}$.
>
> 8 can be divided evenly by 2.   The lowest common denominator is 8.

(2) Multiply the denominators to get a common denominator.

> Find the lowest common denominator for $\frac{1}{2}$ and $\frac{1}{3}$.
>
> Multiply the denominators $3 \times 2 = 6$.   The lowest common denominator is 6.

(3) Go through the multiplication facts of the largest denominator.

> Find the lowest common denominator for $\frac{2}{3}$, $\frac{5}{6}$, and $\frac{1}{9}$.
>
> 9 is the largest denominator.   3 divides evenly into 9, but 6 does not.
> $9 \times 2 = 18$. Both 3 and 6 divide evenly into 18.
> 18 is the lowest common denominator.

Exercise 2

Find the lowest common denominator for each set of fractions. Then change the fractions to equivalent fractions with the common denominator.

1. $\frac{1}{2}$ and $\frac{1}{4}$ _____

2. $\frac{1}{3}$ and $\frac{1}{6}$ _____

3. $\frac{1}{4}$ and $\frac{2}{3}$ _____

4. $\frac{2}{5}$ and $\frac{1}{3}$ _____

5. $\frac{3}{4}$ and $\frac{2}{5}$ _____

6. $\frac{3}{10}$ and $\frac{4}{5}$ _____

7. $\frac{5}{9}, \frac{1}{6}$, and $\frac{7}{12}$ _____

8. $\frac{1}{4}, \frac{3}{7}$, and $\frac{1}{2}$ _____

9. $\frac{4}{15}, \frac{3}{5}$, and $\frac{5}{6}$ _____

Check your answers on page 196.

Reducing Fractions

The same amount is shaded in each of these rectangles. $\frac{4}{8}$ of the
top rectangle is shaded, and $\frac{1}{2}$ of the bottom rectangle is shaded.
The fractions $\frac{4}{8}$ and $\frac{1}{2}$ are equivalent.

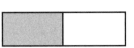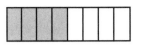

Often you can **reduce** a fraction to an equivalent fraction.
To reduce a fraction, find a number that divides evenly into both the numerator and the
denominator.

Reduce the fraction $\frac{4}{8}$.

$\frac{4 \div 4}{8 \div 4} = \frac{1}{2}$ 4 divides evenly into both 4 and 8. $\frac{4}{8}$ reduces to $\frac{1}{2}$.

To reduce a fraction to its **lowest terms** means to divide both the numerator and the
denominator until they can no longer be divided evenly.

Reduce $\frac{8}{24}$ to its lowest terms.

$\frac{8 \div 8}{24 \div 8} = \frac{1}{3}$ Think about numbers that divide evenly into both 8 and 24.
The numbers 2, 4, and 8 all divide evenly into both 8 and 24.
The largest number, 8, reduces the fraction to lowest terms.
The fraction $\frac{8}{24}$ reduces to $\frac{1}{3}$.

Math Note

You may reduce a fraction by using several steps: $\frac{8}{24} = \frac{4}{12} = \frac{2}{6} = \frac{1}{3}$.

Exercise 3

Reduce each fraction to lowest terms.

1. $\frac{3}{6} =$ 3. $\frac{8}{16} =$ 5. $\frac{16}{24} =$ 7. $\frac{18}{24} =$ 9. $\frac{15}{45} =$

2. $\frac{6}{16} =$ 4. $\frac{6}{18} =$ 6. $\frac{12}{20} =$ 8. $\frac{24}{36} =$ 10. $\frac{20}{36} =$

Check your answers on page 196.

Fractions = Decimals

A fraction and a decimal can represent the same amount. The decimal 0.1 is read as "one tenth." One tenth can also be written as the fraction $\frac{1}{10}$.

To change a decimal to a fraction, write the digits in the decimal as the numerator. Then write the name of the last decimal place as the denominator. Reduce if possible.

> Change 0.5 to a fraction and reduce. $\quad$ $0.5 = \text{five tenths} = \frac{5}{10}$
>
> $\frac{5 \div 5}{10 \div 5} = \frac{1}{2}$ $\quad$ Reduce by dividing the numerator and the denominator by 5.

Exercise 4

Write each decimal as a fraction, and reduce to lowest terms.

1. $0.8 =$ $\qquad$ 2. $0.25 =$ $\qquad$ 3. $0.6 =$ $\qquad$ 4. $0.75 =$ $\qquad$ 5. $0.04 =$

Check your answers on page 196.

Think of a fraction as a division problem. The fraction $\frac{1}{2}$ means 1 divided by 2.

To change a fraction to an equivalent decimal, divide the numerator by the denominator. You will need to write one or more zeros to the right of the decimal point.

> Change $\frac{1}{2}$ to a decimal.
>
> $2\overline{)1.0}$ $\;= 0.5$ $\quad$ Divide the numerator by the denominator.
> Write a zero in the tenths place.
> Place the decimal point in the answer directly above the decimal point in the dividend.
>
> $\frac{1}{2} = 0.5$

Exercise 5

Change each fraction to a decimal. Round repeating decimals to the nearest thousandth.

1. $\frac{1}{4} =$ $\qquad$ 2. $\frac{1}{8} =$ $\qquad$ 3. $\frac{5}{6} =$ $\qquad$ 4. $\frac{3}{5} =$ $\qquad$ 5. $\frac{7}{20} =$

Check your answers on page 196.

Mixed Numbers = Improper Fractions

A mixed number can be changed to an equivalent improper fraction. For example, $2\frac{1}{4}$ is the same as $\frac{9}{4}$.

Exercise 6

Write the mixed number and the improper fraction that represent the shaded portion of each diagram.

    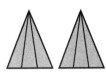

1. _____ = _____   2. _____ = _____   3. _____ = _____

Check your answers on page 196.

To change a mixed number to an improper fraction, first change the whole number to an improper fraction. Then add the fraction. Think about the next example carefully.

Change $2\frac{1}{4}$ to an improper fraction.

$2 = \frac{8}{4}$ Multiply the denominator, 4, by the whole number, 2.

$\frac{8}{4} + \frac{1}{4} = \frac{9}{4}$ Add $\frac{8}{4}$ and $\frac{1}{4}$.

$2\frac{1}{4} = \frac{9}{4}$

You do not have to write all the steps in the last example. To change a mixed number to an improper fraction, multiply the denominator by the whole number. Then add the numerator of the fraction to the product. Finally, write the total over the denominator.

Exercise 7

Change each mixed number to an improper fraction.

1. $4\frac{1}{4} =$ ___   3. $1\frac{2}{3} =$ ___   5. $3\frac{1}{2} =$ ___   7. $2\frac{1}{3} =$ ___   9. $2\frac{5}{6} =$ ___

2. $2\frac{1}{2} =$ ___   4. $1\frac{3}{4} =$ ___   6. $4\frac{2}{5} =$ ___   8. $3\frac{7}{8} =$ ___   10. $1\frac{7}{12} =$ ___

Check your answers on page 197.

Simplifying Improper Fractions

When the answer to a problem is an improper fraction, you usually need to **simplify** the fraction. Change the improper fraction to a whole number or mixed number.

Change $\frac{9}{2}$ to a mixed number.

$$4\frac{1}{2}$$
$$2\overline{)9}$$
$$\underline{-8}$$
$$1$$

Divide the numerator by the denominator.
Write the remainder as a numerator and the divisor as the denominator. $\frac{9}{2} = 4\frac{1}{2}$

Exercise 8

Change the improper fractions to whole numbers or mixed numbers. Reduce all fractions to their lowest terms.

1. $\frac{4}{2} =$ 2. $\frac{10}{10} =$ 3. $\frac{10}{3} =$ 4. $\frac{25}{6} =$ 5. $\frac{13}{8} =$

Check your answers on page 197.

To change an improper fraction to a mixed decimal, divide the numerator by the denominator. Write a decimal point and zeros to the right of the numerator. (To review dividing decimals, see page 116.)

Change $\frac{9}{2}$ to a mixed decimal.

$$4.5$$
$$2\overline{)9.0}$$

Divide the numerator by the denominator.
Write a zero to the right of the decimal point.
$$\frac{9}{2} = 4.5$$

Exercise 9

Change each fraction to an equivalent decimal. Round repeating decimals to the nearest thousandth.

1. $\frac{9}{4} =$ 2. $\frac{7}{2} =$ 3. $\frac{12}{5} =$ 4. $\frac{7}{4} =$ 5. $\frac{25}{6} =$

Check your answers on page 197.

Fractions Checkup

Write the missing numerators in each set of equivalent fractions.

1. $\dfrac{3}{4} = \dfrac{}{8} = \dfrac{}{12} = \dfrac{}{16} = \dfrac{}{20}$

2. $\dfrac{2}{3} = \dfrac{}{6} = \dfrac{}{9} = \dfrac{}{12} = \dfrac{}{15}$

3. $\dfrac{4}{5} = \dfrac{}{10} = \dfrac{}{15} = \dfrac{}{20} = \dfrac{}{25}$

For each set of fractions, write equivalent fractions with the lowest common denominator.

4. $\dfrac{3}{5}$ and $\dfrac{1}{3}$ _____

5. $\dfrac{1}{2}$ and $\dfrac{7}{8}$ _____

6. $\dfrac{3}{4}, \dfrac{5}{6},$ and $\dfrac{3}{8}$ _____

Reduce these fractions to their lowest terms.

7. $\dfrac{8}{16} =$ _____

8. $\dfrac{3}{12} =$ _____

9. $\dfrac{21}{24} =$ _____

Change these mixed numbers to improper fractions.

10. $2\dfrac{1}{2} =$ _____

11. $3\dfrac{3}{4} =$ _____

12. $4\dfrac{1}{5} =$ _____

Change these improper fractions to mixed numbers.

13. $\dfrac{15}{4} =$ _____

14. $\dfrac{9}{5} =$ _____

15. $\dfrac{14}{3} =$ _____

Change these fractions or mixed numbers to decimal form.

16. $\dfrac{2}{5} =$ _____

17. $1\dfrac{3}{8} =$ _____

18. $5\dfrac{1}{2} =$ _____

Check your answers on page 197.

Points to Remember

- Equivalent fractions have the same value.

- To write an equivalent fraction with a larger denominator, multiply both the numerator and the denominator by the same number.

- To reduce a fraction, divide both the numerator and the denominator by the same number.

- To change a fraction to a decimal, divide the numerator of the fraction by the denominator.

Chapter 14

Calculating with Fractions

In daily life, we often use fractions and mixed numbers.

We use them when we go grocery shopping. We read them on packages of food and on scales when we weigh fruits or vegetables. In what other ways do you use fractions and mixed numbers while shopping for food?

We use fractions when we talk about time. We say we will do something in a $\frac{1}{4}$ of an hour, for example. We also use fractions when we talk about longer periods of time, such as $1\frac{1}{2}$ years.

When stores have sales, they may use fractions to show how much prices are discounted. Think about the sale signs advertising $\frac{1}{2}$ off, $\frac{1}{3}$ off, or $\frac{1}{4}$ off.

In this chapter, you will learn the basic skills needed to add, subtract, multiply, and divide fractions and mixed numbers.

Talk Math

Do these activities with a partner or a group.

1. Describe a situation in which you need to use fractions or mixed numbers.
2. With a partner, take turns describing where you have seen fractions used.

Adding Fractions

You add numbers to find a total. When you add fractions, the denominators must be alike. Write an addition problem with fractions horizontally (with the fractions written side by side). Fractions are easier to add this way. Add only the numerators. The sum will have the same denominator as the fractions in the problem.

A cookie recipe calls for $\frac{1}{4}$ cup of whole wheat flour, $\frac{1}{4}$ cup of oat flour, and $\frac{1}{4}$ cup of white flour. What is the total amount of flour used in the recipe?

$$\frac{1}{4} + \frac{1}{4} + \frac{1}{4} = \frac{3}{4}$$

Add the numerators: $1 + 1 + 1 = 3$.

Write the total over the denominator 4.

The recipe calls for $\frac{3}{4}$ cup of flour.

Simplify the answers to addition problems. Reduce when you can, and change improper fractions to whole numbers or mixed numbers.

Find the sum of $\frac{1}{8} + \frac{5}{8} + \frac{7}{8}$.

$$\frac{1}{8} + \frac{5}{8} + \frac{7}{8} = \frac{13}{8}$$

Add the numerators: $1 + 5 + 7 = 13$.

Write the total over the denominator 8.
Change the improper fraction to a mixed number.

$$\frac{13}{8} = 1\frac{5}{8}$$

The sum is $1\frac{5}{8}$.

Exercise 1

Add each problem, and simplify your answers.

1. $\frac{1}{5} + \frac{3}{5} =$ ___
2. $\frac{3}{4} + \frac{3}{4} =$ ___
3. $\frac{5}{16} + \frac{8}{16} =$ ___
4. $\frac{1}{2} + \frac{1}{2} + \frac{1}{2} =$ ___

Check your answers on page 197.

Adding Fractions with Unlike Denominators

You can add fractions only when the denominators are alike. If the denominators are different, find a common denominator. Then change the fractions to equivalent fractions with a common denominator. (To review common denominators, reread page 136.)

Jack has $\frac{1}{2}$ quart of engine oil in one can. In another can, he has $\frac{1}{4}$ quart of engine oil.

How much oil does he have altogether?

Add $\frac{1}{2} + \frac{1}{4}$.   Since 2 divides evenly into 4, the common denominator is 4.

$\frac{1 \times 2}{2 \times 2} = \frac{2}{4}$ Change $\frac{1}{2}$ to fourths.

$\frac{2}{4} + \frac{1}{4} = \frac{3}{4}$ Add $\frac{2}{4}$ and $\frac{1}{4}$.

Jack has a total of $\frac{3}{4}$ quart of oil.

Exercise 2

Find the lowest common denominator for each problem. Then change the fractions to equivalent fractions with the common denominator. Add and simplify the sums.

1. $\frac{1}{2} + \frac{3}{4} =$ 5. $\frac{3}{5} + \frac{7}{10} =$ 9. $\frac{5}{16} + \frac{3}{4} =$

2. $\frac{1}{3} + \frac{1}{2} =$ 6. $\frac{3}{4} + \frac{1}{6} =$ 10. $\frac{1}{2} + \frac{1}{4} + \frac{7}{8} =$

3. $\frac{4}{5} + \frac{1}{2} =$ 7. $\frac{3}{4} + \frac{1}{3} =$ 11. $\frac{1}{3} + \frac{3}{4} + \frac{5}{12} =$

4. $\frac{3}{8} + \frac{1}{4} =$ 8. $\frac{1}{2} + \frac{7}{8} =$ 12. $\frac{1}{4} + \frac{1}{3} + \frac{1}{2} =$

Check your answers on page 197.

Adding Mixed Numbers

To add mixed numbers, write the problems vertically. Write fractions under fractions and whole numbers under whole numbers. Be sure all the fractions have the same denominator. Add the fractions and then the whole numbers. Simplify the answers.

Find the sum of $2\frac{1}{2}$ and $1\frac{3}{4}$.

$$2\frac{1}{2} = 2\frac{2}{4}$$ 2 divides evenly into 4; the common denominator is 4.

$$+ 1\frac{3}{4} = 1\frac{3}{4}$$ Change $\frac{1}{2}$ to fourths.

$$\phantom{+ 1\frac{3}{4} = } 3\frac{5}{4}$$ Add the fractions and add the whole numbers.

$$3\frac{5}{4} = 3 + 1\frac{1}{4} = 4\frac{1}{4}$$ Change the answer to a mixed number. The sum is $4\frac{1}{4}$.

Check your answer by rounding each mixed number to the nearest whole number.

$$2\frac{1}{2} \text{ and } 1\frac{3}{4} \approx 3 + 2 = 5$$

The estimate, 5, is close to the sum, $4\frac{1}{4}$. The answer is reasonable.

Exercise 3

Estimate each answer by rounding the mixed numbers to the nearest whole numbers and adding the rounded numbers. Then find each exact answer. Simplify each sum.

1. $2\frac{1}{4} + 3\frac{1}{4} =$ 4. $1\frac{1}{2} + 3\frac{7}{8} =$ 7. $4\frac{3}{8} + 2\frac{5}{8} =$ 10. $1\frac{1}{2} + 4\frac{5}{8} =$

2. $4\frac{1}{8} + 2\frac{3}{8} =$ 5. $2\frac{2}{3} + 2\frac{1}{2} =$ 8. $5\frac{1}{2} + 2\frac{5}{6} =$ 11. $6\frac{3}{4} + 4\frac{5}{6} =$

3. $1\frac{7}{10} + 3\frac{1}{2} =$ 6. $4\frac{3}{4} + 3\frac{1}{4} =$ 9. $3\frac{3}{4} + 4\frac{7}{8} =$ 12. $2\frac{2}{3} + 5\frac{1}{2} =$

Check your answers on page 197.

Subtracting Fractions

To subtract fractions, subtract only the numerators. Be sure that each fraction in a problem has the same denominator. Reduce answers to lowest terms.

Subtract $\frac{3}{4} - \frac{1}{4}$.

$\frac{3}{4} - \frac{1}{4} = \frac{2}{4}$ Subtract the numerators and put the difference over 4.

$\frac{2 \div 2}{4 \div 2} = \frac{1}{2}$ Reduce $\frac{2}{4}$ to $\frac{1}{2}$.

Exercise 4

Solve the problems. Reduce each answer to lowest terms.

1. $\frac{2}{3} - \frac{1}{3} =$ ___

2. $\frac{6}{8} - \frac{3}{8} =$ ___

3. $\frac{10}{12} - \frac{3}{12} =$ ___

4. $\frac{9}{10} - \frac{5}{10} =$ ___

Check your answers on page 198.

When the fractions in a subtraction problem have different denominators, you need to find a common denominator. Then change one or both fractions to equivalent fractions with the common denominator.

Subtract $\frac{1}{2} - \frac{1}{3}$.   The common denominator is $2 \times 3 = 6$.

$\frac{1 \times 3}{2 \times 3} = \frac{3}{6}$ $\frac{1 \times 2}{3 \times 2} = \frac{2}{6}$ Change to equivalent fractions with a denominator of 6.

$\frac{3}{6} - \frac{2}{6} = \frac{1}{6}$ Subtract the fractions.

Exercise 5

Solve each problem. Reduce each answer to lowest terms.

1. $\frac{3}{4} - \frac{1}{2} =$

3. $\frac{4}{5} - \frac{3}{10} =$

5. $\frac{5}{8} - \frac{1}{4} =$

7. $\frac{3}{4} - \frac{3}{16} =$

2. $\frac{1}{2} - \frac{1}{3} =$

4. $\frac{2}{3} - \frac{1}{2} =$

6. $\frac{2}{3} - \frac{1}{5} =$

8. $\frac{1}{2} - \frac{5}{12} =$

Check your answers on page 198.

Subtracting Fractions from Whole Numbers

To subtract a fraction from a whole number, borrow 1 from the whole number. Then write the 1 as an improper fraction with the same denominator as the other fraction in the problem.

Ruth plans to walk 2 miles. So far she has walked $\frac{3}{4}$ mile. How many more miles does she need to walk?

$$
\begin{array}{r}
\overset{\scriptstyle 1\,\frac{4}{4}}{\cancel{2}} \\
-\ \frac{3}{4} \\
\hline
1\,\frac{1}{4}
\end{array}
$$

Borrow 1 from 2, and rewrite the 1 as $\frac{4}{4}$.

Subtract the fractions: $\frac{4}{4} - \frac{3}{4} = \frac{1}{4}$.

Subtract the whole numbers: $1 - 0 = 1$.

Ruth needs to walk $1\,\frac{1}{4}$ miles more.

Exercise 6

For each problem, change 1 to an improper fraction. Use the denominator given.

1. thirds
   1 = ____

2. halves
   1 = ____

3. fifths
   1 = ____

4. tenths
   1 = ____

5. eighths
   1 = ____

6. sixteenths
   1 = ____

7. fourths
   1 = ____

8. sixths
   1 = ____

Check your answers on page 198.

Exercise 7

Solve each problem. Reduce each answer to lowest terms.

1. $1 - \frac{2}{3} =$

2. $1 - \frac{3}{4} =$

3. $2 - \frac{3}{8} =$

4. $3 - \frac{4}{5} =$

5. $5 - \frac{3}{4} =$

6. $3 - \frac{9}{10} =$

7. $9 - \frac{1}{2} =$

8. $7 - \frac{2}{3} =$

9. $8 - \frac{1}{2} =$

Check your answers on page 198.

Subtracting Mixed Numbers

To subtract mixed numbers, be sure that the fractions in the problem have a common denominator. Borrow 1 whole if you need to. Subtract the fractions, and then subtract the whole numbers. Reduce answers to lowest terms. Read the next example carefully.

Subtract $4\frac{1}{4} - 2\frac{3}{8}$.   8 is the common denominator.

$\frac{1 \times 2}{4 \times 2} = \frac{2}{8}$ Change $\frac{1}{4}$ to eighths.

You cannot subtract $\frac{3}{8}$ from $\frac{2}{8}$.

Borrow 1 whole; change 1 to $\frac{8}{8}$; and add it to $\frac{2}{8}$.

$$4\frac{2}{8} = 3\frac{8}{8} + \frac{2}{8} = 3\frac{10}{8}$$

$$\begin{array}{r} 4\frac{2}{8} \\ -2\frac{3}{8} \\ \hline \end{array} \qquad \begin{array}{r} 3\frac{10}{8} \\ -2\frac{3}{8} \\ \hline 1\frac{7}{8} \end{array}$$ Subtract the fractions and the whole numbers.

To check your answer, round every mixed number to the nearest whole number.

$$4\frac{1}{4} - 2\frac{3}{8} \approx 4 - 2 = 2$$

The estimate, 2, is close to the difference, $1\frac{7}{8}$. The answer is reasonable.

Exercise 8

For each problem, first estimate the difference by rounding the mixed numbers to the nearest whole numbers and subtracting the rounded numbers. Then find each exact answer. Reduce the answers to lowest terms.

1. $2\frac{2}{3} - 1\frac{1}{3} =$

2. $4\frac{3}{4} - 2\frac{1}{4} =$

3. $2\frac{4}{5} - 1\frac{3}{5} =$

4. $5\frac{1}{2} - 1\frac{1}{4} =$

5. $4\frac{1}{2} - 1\frac{3}{8} =$

6. $5\frac{1}{2} - 2\frac{1}{3} =$

7. $8\frac{1}{4} - 3\frac{3}{4} =$

8. $7\frac{1}{5} - 4\frac{3}{5} =$

9. $6\frac{1}{2} - 3\frac{2}{3} =$

10. $4 - 2\frac{1}{2} =$

11. $7\frac{5}{8} - 5\frac{1}{2} =$

12. $9\frac{1}{4} - 7\frac{1}{2} =$

Check your answers on page 198.

148   **Chapter 14** *Calculating with Fractions*

Multiplying Fractions

When you see the phrase "a fraction of," you must multiply to solve the problem. When you find a fraction of a number, the answer will be smaller than the original number. To multiply fractions, first multiply the numerators, and then multiply the denominators. Reduce the answer to lowest terms.

A recipe calls for a $\frac{1}{2}$ cup of milk. If Maria wants to make only $\frac{1}{2}$ of this recipe, how much milk will she need?

$\frac{1}{2}$ of $\frac{1}{2}$ cup =   The problems asks for $\frac{1}{2}$ of $\frac{1}{2}$, or $\frac{1}{2} \times \frac{1}{2}$.

$\frac{1}{2} \times \frac{1}{2} = \frac{1}{4}$ Multiply the numerators, and multiply the denominators.

The product is $\frac{1}{4}$.

Maria needs $\frac{1}{4}$ cup of milk.

Exercise 9

Set up and solve each problem. Reduce the answers to lowest terms.

1. $\frac{1}{2}$ of $\frac{3}{4}$ yard of fabric
Problem:

3. $\frac{1}{3}$ of $\frac{9}{10}$ mile
Problem:

5. $\frac{1}{4}$ of $\frac{1}{4}$ pound of cheese
Problem:

2. $\frac{1}{4}$ of $\frac{1}{2}$ gallon of milk
Problem:

4. $\frac{1}{2}$ of $\frac{1}{2}$ of a dollar
Problem:

6. $\frac{1}{3}$ of $\frac{3}{4}$ hour
Problem:

7. $\frac{2}{3} \times \frac{3}{4} =$

9. $\frac{3}{10} \times \frac{1}{6} =$

11. $\frac{5}{8} \times \frac{2}{3} =$

8. $\frac{5}{6} \times \frac{3}{8} =$

10. $\frac{3}{4} \times \frac{4}{5} =$

12. $\frac{5}{6} \times \frac{7}{10} =$

Check your answers on page 198.

Canceling

Canceling is a shortcut for multiplying fractions. Canceling is similar to reducing. Divide a numerator and a denominator in a problem by the same number. Then multiply by the new numbers.

Use canceling to find the product of $\frac{3}{8} \times \frac{2}{5}$.

$$\frac{3}{\overset{}{\underset{4}{8}}} \times \frac{\overset{1}{2}}{5} = \frac{3}{20}$$

Divide both 2 and 8 by 2.

Multiply the new numerators: $3 \times 1 = 3$.

Multiply the new denominators: $4 \times 5 = 20$.

The product is $\frac{3}{20}$.

Sometimes you can cancel more than once. Look at this example carefully.

Use canceling to find the product of $\frac{8}{15} \times \frac{5}{12}$.

$$\frac{\overset{2}{8}}{\underset{3}{15}} \times \frac{\overset{1}{5}}{\underset{3}{12}} = \frac{2}{9}$$

Divide both 8 and 12 by 4.

Divide both 5 and 15 by 5.

Multiply the new numerators: $2 \times 1 = 2$.

Multiply the new denominators: $3 \times 3 = 9$.

The product is $\frac{2}{9}$.

After you cancel and multiply the new numerators and the new denominators, check your answer. Be sure the answer is reduced to lowest terms.

Exercise 10

Use canceling to solve each problem.

1. $\frac{5}{8} \times \frac{3}{10} =$

2. $\frac{7}{12} \times \frac{8}{9} =$

3. $\frac{2}{3} \times \frac{9}{10} =$

4. $\frac{3}{4} \times \frac{2}{5} =$

5. $\frac{6}{7} \times \frac{7}{8} =$

6. $\frac{9}{32} \times \frac{8}{15} =$

7. $\frac{5}{16} \times \frac{4}{5} =$

8. $\frac{9}{10} \times \frac{5}{6} =$

9. $\frac{5}{12} \times \frac{8}{25} =$

10. $\frac{1}{2} \times \frac{8}{9} =$

11. $\frac{15}{16} \times \frac{3}{5} =$

12. $\frac{9}{20} \times \frac{2}{3} =$

Check your answers on page 199.

A Fraction of a Whole Number

To find a fraction of a whole number, change the whole number to an improper fraction. Then multiply the numerators and the denominators.

Ellen estimates that it will take 6 hours to pack everything in her kitchen. The movers she hired estimate $\frac{3}{4}$ of that time. How long do the movers think it will take?

$\frac{3}{4} \times 6 =$ Set up a multiplication problem.

$\frac{3}{4} \times \frac{6}{1} =$ Change 6 to an improper fraction with a denominator of 1.

$\frac{3}{4} \times \frac{6}{1} = \frac{18}{4}$ Multiply the numerators and multiply the denominators.

$\frac{18}{4} = \frac{9}{2} = 4\frac{1}{2}$ Simplify the answer.

The movers think they will need $4\frac{1}{2}$ hours.

When the answer is an improper fraction, change it to a whole number or a mixed number. Reduce fractions to lowest terms.

Exercise 11

Solve each problem, and simplify the answers.

1. $\frac{3}{4} \times 8 =$

2. $\frac{2}{3} \times 12 =$

3. $\frac{3}{4} \times 9 =$

4. $\frac{1}{2} \times 15 =$

5. $\frac{1}{4} \times 5 =$

6. $\frac{2}{3} \times 9 =$

7. $\frac{4}{5} \times 12 =$

8. $\frac{3}{10} \times 8 =$

9. $\frac{3}{4} \times 7 =$

10. $\frac{2}{3} \times 15 =$

11. $\frac{3}{8} \times 12 =$

12. $\frac{2}{5} \times 10 =$

Check your answers on page 199.

A Fraction of a Mixed Number

To find a fraction of a mixed number, first change the mixed number to an improper fraction. (Review this on page 139.) Then multiply numerators and denominators.

Jennifer lost $8\frac{1}{2}$ pounds. If she lost $\frac{1}{4}$ of that amount in one week, how many pounds did she lose that week?

$\frac{1}{4} \times 8\frac{1}{2} =$ Set up a multiplication problem.

$\frac{1}{4} \times \frac{17}{2} =$ Change $8\frac{1}{2}$ to an improper fraction.

$\frac{1}{4} \times \frac{17}{2} = \frac{17}{8}$ Multiply the numerators and the denominators.

$\frac{17}{8} = 2\frac{1}{8}$ Simplify the answer. Jennifer lost $2\frac{1}{8}$ pounds that week.

To check your answer, round the mixed number to the nearest whole number.

$$\frac{1}{4} \times 8\frac{1}{2} \approx \frac{1}{4} \times 9 = \frac{9}{4} = 2\frac{1}{4}$$

The estimate, $2\frac{1}{4}$, is close to the answer, $2\frac{1}{8}$. The answer is reasonable.

Exercise 12

First estimate each problem by rounding each mixed number to the nearest whole number and finding the product with the rounded number. Then find the exact answer to each problem and simplify the answers.

1. $\frac{1}{2} \times 1\frac{1}{2} =$ 3. $\frac{1}{4} \times 4\frac{3}{4} =$ 5. $\frac{2}{3} \times 6\frac{1}{3} =$ 7. $\frac{1}{3} \times 5\frac{1}{4} =$

2. $\frac{1}{3} \times 3\frac{1}{2} =$ 4. $\frac{3}{4} \times 5\frac{1}{2} =$ 6. $\frac{1}{2} \times 7\frac{1}{4} =$ 8. $\frac{1}{2} \times 6\frac{3}{4} =$

Check your answers on page 199.

Dividing by a Fraction

Think about each of these pairs of problems.

$$8 \div 2 = 4 \quad \text{and} \quad 8 \times \frac{1}{2} = 4 \qquad\qquad 6 \div 3 = 2 \quad \text{and} \quad 6 \times \frac{1}{3} = 2$$

For each pair, the answer to the division problem is the same as the answer to a similar multiplication problem.

Use multiplication to divide by a fraction. The first step is to **invert** the divisor.

The inverse of $\frac{2}{3}$ is $\frac{3}{2}$.　　　　The inverse of $\frac{1}{2}$ is $\frac{2}{1}$.

The **inverse** of a number is sometimes called the **reciprocal**. Notice that in the inverse, the numerator and the denominator trade places.

Exercise 13

Write the inverse for each fraction.

1. $\frac{1}{2}$ ___　　　2. $\frac{3}{4}$ ___　　　3. $\frac{5}{8}$ ___　　　4. $\frac{3}{10}$ ___　　　5. $\frac{7}{16}$ ___

Check your answers on page 199.

To divide by a fraction, invert the divisor, and change the $\div$ sign to a $\times$ sign. Then follow the rules for multiplying fractions.

Find the quotient of $5 \div \frac{3}{4}$.

$5 \div \frac{3}{4} =$	Invert the divisor $\frac{3}{4}$ and change the $\div$ sign to a $\times$ sign.
$5 \times \frac{4}{3} =$	The inverse of $\frac{3}{4}$ is $\frac{4}{3}$.
$\frac{5}{1} \times \frac{4}{3} = \frac{20}{3}$	Write 5 as the improper fraction $\frac{5}{1}$ and multiply.
$\frac{20}{3} = 6\frac{2}{3}$	Simplify the answer. The quotient is $6\frac{2}{3}$.

Exercise 14

In each problem, first change the whole number or the mixed number to an improper fraction. Then solve each problem and simplify the answers.

1. $9 \div \frac{3}{4} =$　　　3. $3\frac{1}{2} \div \frac{5}{8} =$　　　5. $2\frac{1}{4} \div \frac{5}{6} =$　　　7. $3\frac{3}{4} \div \frac{3}{5} =$

2. $4\frac{2}{3} \div \frac{1}{3} =$　　　4. $6\frac{3}{4} \div \frac{3}{4} =$　　　6. $10 \div \frac{2}{5} =$　　　8. $7 \div \frac{3}{4} =$

Check your answers on page 199.

Dividing by Whole Numbers or Mixed Numbers

When the divisor in a fraction problem is a whole number or a mixed number, first change the divisor to an improper fraction.

What is the reciprocal of 4?	What is the reciprocal $3\frac{2}{3}$?
$4 = \frac{4}{1}$ The reciprocal of $\frac{4}{1}$ is $\frac{1}{4}$.	$3\frac{2}{3} = \frac{11}{3}$ The reciprocal of $\frac{11}{3}$ is $\frac{3}{11}$.

Exercise 15

Change each number to an improper fraction. Then write the reciprocal.

1. $3\frac{1}{2} =$ ____

   reciprocal: ____

2. $4\frac{2}{3} =$ ____

   reciprocal: ____

3. $1\frac{5}{8} =$ ____

   reciprocal: ____

4. $8 =$ ____

   reciprocal: ____

Check your answers on page 199.

To solve a division problem with fractions, first invert the divisor and change the $\div$ sign to a $\times$ sign. Then follow the rules for multiplication.

Find the quotient of $5\frac{1}{2} \div 4$.

$\frac{11}{2} \div \frac{4}{1} =$ Write both numbers as improper fractions.

$\frac{11}{2} \times \frac{1}{4} =$ Invert the divisor $\frac{4}{1}$ and change the $\div$ sign to a $\times$ sign.

$\frac{11}{2} \times \frac{1}{4} = \frac{11}{8}$ Multiply the numerators and the denominators.

$\frac{11}{8} = 1\frac{3}{8}$ Simplify the answer. The quotient is $1\frac{3}{8}$.

Exercise 16

First estimate each answer by rounding each fraction or mixed number to the nearest whole number. Divide the rounded numbers. Then find each exact answer.

1. $2\frac{1}{2} \div 2 =$

2. $1\frac{3}{4} \div 4 =$

3. $4\frac{2}{3} \div 1\frac{1}{3} =$

4. $6\frac{1}{2} \div 1\frac{1}{2} =$

5. $\frac{3}{4} \div 3 =$

6. $\frac{1}{2} \div 5 =$

7. $8\frac{3}{4} \div 1\frac{1}{4} =$

8. $\frac{2}{3} \div 1\frac{1}{3} =$

Check your answers on page 199.

Fractions Word Problems

Review the strategy for solving word problems on page 72 before doing this exercise.

Exercise 17

First estimate each answer. Round each mixed number to the nearest whole number and solve the problem with the rounded numbers. Then find the exact answer.

1. Georgia bought $2\frac{3}{4}$ yards of material that cost $12 per yard. How much did she pay?

Estimate	Exact

2. Fred drives $1\frac{1}{2}$ miles to take his son to school. Then he drives $4\frac{3}{4}$ miles to get to his job. What is the total distance he drives?

Estimate	Exact

3. To paint his garage, Jude bought 6 gallons of paint. So far he has used $4\frac{1}{3}$ gallons. How much paint does he have left?

Estimate	Exact

4. Martha drove $3\frac{1}{2}$ hours at an average speed of 64 miles per hour. How far did she drive?

Estimate	Exact

5. How many shelves each $1\frac{1}{2}$ feet long can Alex cut from a board that is 9 feet long?

Estimate	Exact

6. John is $69\frac{1}{2}$ inches tall. His son Sam is $3\frac{1}{2}$ inches taller. How tall is Sam?

Estimate	Exact

Check your answers on page 199.

Points to Remember

- To add or subtract fractions, the fractions must have the same denominators. Change denominators to a common denominator.

- To multiply fractions, multiply both the numerators and the denominators.

- To divide fractions, invert the divisor and change the ÷ sign to a × sign. Then follow the rules for multiplying.

Fractions Checkup

Solve each problem. Simplify all answers.

1. $\dfrac{1}{8} + \dfrac{5}{8} =$

2. $\dfrac{2}{3} + \dfrac{3}{5} =$

3. $1\dfrac{1}{2} + 2\dfrac{3}{4} =$

4. $1 - \dfrac{1}{4} =$

5. $\dfrac{5}{8} - \dfrac{1}{2} =$

6. $6\dfrac{1}{3} - 2\dfrac{2}{3} =$

7. $\dfrac{1}{2} \times \dfrac{3}{4} =$

8. $\dfrac{4}{5} \times 2\dfrac{1}{2} =$

9. $1\dfrac{1}{4} \times 8 =$

10. $\dfrac{3}{4} \div \dfrac{5}{6} =$

11. $5 \div \dfrac{1}{2} =$

12. $3\dfrac{1}{4} \div 2 =$

For each problem, first estimate an answer. Round each mixed number to the nearest whole number, and solve the problem with the rounded numbers. Then find the exact answer.

13. From a piece of wood trim that was 30 inches long, Shirley cut a piece that was $15\dfrac{3}{4}$ inches long. How long was the remaining piece of trim?

Estimate	Exact

14. By the end of last year, the citizens of Pleasantville had raised $\$2\dfrac{1}{2}$ million to pay for a new community center. So far this year they have raised another $\$1\dfrac{3}{10}$ million. How much do they have altogether?

Estimate	Exact

15. Find the price of a piece of cheese that weighs $3\dfrac{1}{8}$ pounds if the cost is $\$8.40$ per pound.

Estimate	Exact

16. A cardboard box is designed to hold 20 pounds of books. How many reference books each weighing $2\dfrac{1}{2}$ pounds can one of the boxes hold?

Estimate	Exact

Check your answers on page 200.

UNIT 5

Ratio and Percent

In this unit, you will learn the basic skills needed to work with ratio and percent. You will learn how to

- write ratios and proportions

- use ratio and percent to compare amounts

- change percents to equivalent fractions and decimals

- use a proportion to solve for an unknown amount

- calculate a percent of a number

- find what percent one number is of another

Chapter 15

Ratio Basics

One way to compare two numbers is to subtract.

For example, a pair of gloves is on sale for $10. The regular price of the gloves is $15. You can subtract to compare the regular price and the sale price.

$$\$15 - \$10 = \$5 \longleftarrow \text{difference}$$

The sale price of the gloves is $5 less than the regular price.

Another way to compare two numbers is to express a ratio. A **ratio** uses division to compare two numbers.

For example, a ratio can be used to compare two prices. The ratio of the sale price of the gloves to the regular price is $10 to $15. You can write the ratio as

$10 to $15 or **10 : 15** or $\dfrac{10}{15}$.

Ratios are also used to express **rates**. A rate compares a number of units of one measurement to a single unit of another measurement—for example, dollars per year or miles per hour. Here are two examples of rates.

Annual salary
Ratio: $22,000 to 1 year

Speed limit
Raito: 55 miles to 1 hour

Talk Math

Do these activities with a partner or a group.

1. Describe situations in which you compare two amounts by using ratios.
2. Take turns naming a ratio and discussing what is being compared. For example, you might say, "12 to 17." Your partner could say, "12 men to 17 women in my class."

Writing Ratios

A ratio can be expressed with the word *to* as in **1 to 2**, or with a colon (:) as in **1 : 2**, or as a fraction such as $\frac{1}{2}$. Read each of these ratios as "1 to 2."

Each number in a ratio is called a **term**. Write the terms in a ratio in the order stated in the question.

A shop has five employees. Three of the employees are women. What is the ratio of the number of women to the total number of employees?   women : total = 3 : 5

In the example, the answer is 3 : 5, *not* 5 : 3. The ratio 5 : 3 would be the ratio of the total number of employees to the number of women.

Exercise 1

Write each ratio using the word *to*.

1. A baseball team has 9 players, and a football team has 11 players. What is the ratio of the number of players on a baseball team to the number of players on a football team? _____

2. In Jan's school there are 7 English teachers and 4 science teachers. What is the ratio of the number of science teachers to the number of English teachers? _____

Write each ratio with a colon (:).

3. A paving block is 7 inches wide and 12 inches long. What is the ratio of the width to the length? _____

4. Jed is 28 years old and his son Logan is 5 years old. What is the ratio of Logan's age to Jed's age? _____

Express each ratio as a fraction.

5. A team played 80 games and won 63. Write the ratio of the number of games the team won to the number of games the team played. _____

6. In a yoga class, there are 16 women and 11 men. What is the ratio of the number of men in the class to the number of women? _____

Check your answers on page 200.

Reducing Ratios

A ratio, like a fraction, can be reduced. Reduce a ratio the same way you reduce a fraction. Divide the terms by a number that divides evenly into both terms. (To review reducing fractions, reread page 137.)

> By the end of the baseball season, José had 40 hits for 140 times at bat. What is the ratio of his hits to his times at bat?
>
> $$\frac{40}{140} = \frac{40 \div 10}{140 \div 10} = \frac{4 \div 2}{14 \div 2} = \frac{2}{7}$$
>
> Reduce both terms by 10 and then again by 2. The ratio of hits to times at bat is 2 : 7.

The numerator and the denominator are both divided until they can no longer be divided evenly by the same number. The ratio 40 : 140 reduced to lowest terms is 2 : 7.

Math Note

Reduce ratios that are improper fractions to their lowest terms.

$$\frac{10}{5} = \frac{2}{1} \qquad 10 : 5 = 2 : 1 \qquad 10 \text{ to } 5 = 2 \text{ to } 1$$

Do not change ratios into mixed numbers.

Exercise 2

Reduce each ratio to lowest terms.

1. 4 to 8 = _____
2. 9 : 6 = _____
3. 12 to 4 = _____
4. 32 : 16 = _____
5. 24 : 40 = _____
6. 24 to 48 = _____
7. 45 : 60 = _____
8. 120 to 100 = _____

Exercise 3

Use a colon (:) to write a ratio for each problem. Then simplify each ratio by reducing to lowest terms.

1. Only 3 of the 24 students in Mary's class walk to school. What is the ratio of the number of students who walk to the total number of students? _____

2. 15 out of 25 board members voted no on an important issue. What is the ratio of members who voted no to total members? _____

3. A car traveled 288 miles on 12 gallons. What is the ratio of miles to gallons? _____

Check your answers on page 200.

Rates

A **rate** is a kind of ratio. A rate compares a measurement to a single unit of another measurement. The word *per* (meaning "for each") is often used to express rates. Examples of rates are **28 miles per gallon**, **$15 per hour**, and **35 students per class**.

On a typing test, Ramon typed 225 words in 5 minutes.
Find his typing rate in **words per minute**.

$225 \div 5 = 45$ Divide 225 words by 5 minutes.
Ramon's typing rate is 45 words per minute.

Exercise 4

Use a calculator to solve each problem.

1. A bus traveled 92 miles in 4 hours. What was its speed in miles per hour? _____

2. A seafood restaurant with 42 tables has 7 waiters. If the work is shared equally, how many tables does each server take care of? _____

3. A school has 16 classrooms and 432 students. If all the classrooms are used, find the average number of students per classroom. _____

4. Anna drove 130 miles on 5 gallons of gasoline. Find her gas mileage rate. _____

5. Beth paid $504 for electricity last year. What monthly rate did she pay? (1 year = 12 months) _____

6. A theater has a total of 864 seats, set in 24 equal rows. Find the number of seats per row. _____

7. During 5 minutes on a running machine, Malcolm's heart beat 360 times. Calculate his heartbeats per minute. _____

8. 30 families with 96 children live in the Green Acres housing development. Find the average number of children per family. _____

Check your answers on page 200.

Ratio Word Problems

In ratio problems, you sometimes have to calculate to find one of the terms in the ratio. Read the next example carefully. Remember to write the terms of the ratio in the order they are stated in a problem.

> On a Spanish quiz, Jennifer got 7 questions right and 3 questions wrong. What is the ratio of the number of questions she got right to the total number of questions on the test?
>
> 7 right + 3 wrong = 10 questions   Find the total number of questions.
>
> right : total = 7 : 10   The first term is the number right, 7.
> The second term is the total, 10.

Exercise 5

Use a colon (:) to write a ratio for each problem. Simplify the answers.

1. There are 8 men and 12 women in Mrs. Garcia's Spanish class.
   a. What is the ratio of women to the total number of students? _____
   b. What is the ratio of women to men in the class? _____
   c. What is the ratio of men to the total number of students? _____

2. One season a baseball team played 162 games and won 108 games.
   a. What is the ratio of the number of games the team won to the number of games they lost? _____
   b. What is the ratio of the number of games the team won to the number of games they played? _____
   c. What is the ratio of the number of games the team lost to the number of games they played? _____

3. There are 45 workers at the factory where Margaret works. On the day of a blizzard, 9 workers were absent.
   a. What is the ratio of the number of workers who were absent to the number who came to work the day of the blizzard? _____
   b. What is the ratio of the number of workers who were absent on the day of the blizzard to the total number of workers? _____
   c. What is the ratio of the number of workers who came to work the day of the blizzard to the total number of workers? _____

Check your answers on page 200.

Proportion

Two equivalent ratios are called a **proportion**. Express a proportion by writing an equals sign (=) between the equivalent ratios.

Each rectangle below equals 1 whole. The ratio of the shaded parts to the whole is the same in both rectangles.

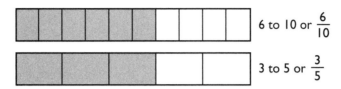

6 to 10 or $\frac{6}{10}$

3 to 5 or $\frac{3}{5}$

In one rectangle, 6 out of 10 parts are shaded. In the other rectangle, 3 out of 5 parts are shaded. The ratio of 6 to 10 is the same as the ratio of 3 to 5.

You can write the ratios in a proportion with colons (:) or with fractions.

$$6 : 10 = 3 : 5 \qquad or \qquad \frac{6}{10} = \frac{3}{5}$$

Read the proportion as "6 to 10 is the same as 3 to 5."

A proportion has two **cross products**. A cross product is the product of the numerator of one ratio times the denominator of the other ratio. The two cross products are always equal.

Write the cross products for the proportion $\frac{6}{10} = \frac{3}{5}$.

$$\frac{6}{10} \bowtie \frac{3}{5}$$

$6 \times 5 = 30$ ←—— cross product

$10 \times 3 = 30$ ←—— cross product

Exercise 6

Write the two cross products for each proportion.

1. $\frac{2}{3} = \frac{8}{12}$

   a. _____

   b. _____

2. $\frac{3}{4} = \frac{12}{16}$

   a. _____

   b. _____

3. $\frac{1}{6} = \frac{5}{30}$

   a. _____

   b. _____

4. $\frac{7}{10} = \frac{28}{40}$

   a. _____

   b. _____

5. $\frac{5}{20} = \frac{2}{8}$

   a. _____

   b. _____

6. $\frac{16}{24} = \frac{2}{3}$

   a. _____

   b. _____

7. $\frac{9}{12} = \frac{12}{16}$

   a. _____

   b. _____

8. $\frac{5}{10} = \frac{9}{18}$

   a. _____

   b. _____

Check your answers on page 200.

Solving for an Unknown

You can use a proportion to solve for an unknown term. A letter is used to represent the unknown term.

To solve a proportion with an unknown term, first write an equation with the cross products. Then divide both cross products by the number with the unknown.

Solve for the unknown term in the proportion $\dfrac{3}{4} = \dfrac{9}{m}$.

$3 \times m = 36$	One cross product is $3 \times m$; the other product is $4 \times 9 = 36$.
$m = 12$	Divide both sides of the equation by 3.
	The value of the missing term is $m = 12$.

To check whether the unknown is correct, find both cross products. If the cross products are equal, the answer is correct. $3 \times 12 = 36$ and $4 \times 9 = 36$.

Solve for the unknown term in the proportion $\dfrac{12}{n} = \dfrac{4}{6}$.

$4 \times n = 72$	One cross product is $4 \times n$; the other product is $12 \times 6 = 72$.
$n = 18$	Divide both sides of the equation by 4.
	The value of the missing term is $n = 18$.

Check to see if the cross products are equal. $12 \times 6 = 72$ and $18 \times 4 = 72$.

Exercise 7

Solve for each unknown. Then check each answer. Use the value of the unknown to find out whether the cross products are equal.

1. $\dfrac{3}{5} = \dfrac{u}{15}$ 3. $\dfrac{g}{5} = \dfrac{6}{15}$ 5. $\dfrac{1.5}{3} = \dfrac{r}{6}$ 7. $\dfrac{7}{e} = \dfrac{35}{100}$

2. $\dfrac{x}{3} = \dfrac{9}{27}$ 4. $\dfrac{4}{a} = \dfrac{16}{20}$ 6. $\dfrac{5}{9} = \dfrac{x}{18}$ 8. $\dfrac{4}{n} = \dfrac{80}{180}$

Check your answers on page 200.

Proportion Word Problems

To solve for an unknown term in a proportion word problem, first be sure that the terms in each ratio correspond. For example, if the ratio on the left represents men to women, the ratio on the right must also represent men to women.

A cake recipe calls for 2 cups of sugar for every 3 cups of flour. Barbara increased the amount of flour to 6 cups. How much sugar should she use?

$$\frac{2}{3} = \frac{s}{6}$$ Write a proportion with the ratio **sugar : flour** on each side.
Let s represent the unknown amount of sugar.

$3 \times s = 12$ Find the cross products.

$s = 4$ Divide by 3. Barbara needs 4 cups of sugar.

To check the answer, multiply the cross products. If the two cross products are equal, the answer is correct. $2 \times 6 = 12$ and $3 \times 4 = 12$.

Exercise 8

Use a proportion to find the unknown. Let x stand for the unknown term.

1. The ratio of the number of men to the number of women in a factory is 5 : 2. There are 40 women working there. How many men work there?

2. A photograph is 3 inches wide and 5 inches long. If the photograph is enlarged to make a poster that is 30 inches long, how wide will the poster be?

3. Anna drove 208 miles on 8 gallons of gas. At that rate, how far can she drive with 12 gallons of gas?

4. Sam makes $25 for 2 hours of overtime work. How much will he make for 4.5 hours of overtime?

5. In 3 hours Pat drove 174 miles. If she drives at the same rate, how far can she go in 5 hours?

6. In the Pleasant Meadows housing development, 3 out of 5 households have children in the public school system. There are 270 households in the development. How many of the households have children in the public school system?

Check your answers on page 200.

Exercise 9

1. On a final exam, Kathy got 1 problem wrong for every 9 problems that she got right.
   a. What is the ratio of the number of problems Kathy got right to the number she got wrong? _____
   b. What is the ratio of the number of problems Kathy got wrong to the total number of problems? _____
   c. What is the ratio of the number of problems Kathy got right to the total number of problems? _____
   d. Kathy got a total of 180 problems right. How many problems were on the test? _____

2. The ratio of men to women in Mr. Martin's English classes is 3 : 5.
   a. What is the ratio of the number of women to the number of men in the classes? _____
   b. What is the ratio of the number of men to the total number of students in the classes? _____
   c. What is the ratio of the number of women to the total number of students in the classes? _____
   d. In Mr. Martin's classes there are 96 students. How many women are in his classes? _____

Check your answers on page 200.

Points to Remember

- A ratio uses division to compare two numbers.

- Fractions are ratios. A ratio is usually expressed in lowest terms.

- A rate is a ratio in which a measurement in one unit is compared to a single unit of another measurement.

- A proportion is an equation made up of two ratios. The cross products of a proportion are equal.

Ratio Checkup

1. A magazine is 9 inches wide and 12 inches long. Write and simplify the ratio of the width to the length. _____

2. There were 20 questions on Linda's Spanish test, and she got 16 of them correct. Write and simplify the ratio of the number of questions Linda got right to the number of questions on the test. _____

3. Manny works 50 weeks every year and has a 2-week vacation. Write and simplify the ratio of the weeks Manny works to the weeks he is on vacation. _____

4. Silvia typed 180 words in 4 minutes. What was her typing rate in words per minute? _____

5. Chris drove 46 miles on 2 gallons of gasoline. What was his gas use in miles per gallon? _____

6. At night school, 96 students use 3 classrooms. Find the average number of students per class. _____

7. One season a team won 120 games and lost 30 games.

    a. Write and simplify the ratio of the number of games won to the number they lost. _____

    b. Write and simplify the ratio of the number of games won to the number of games played.

    _____

    c. Write and simplify the ratio of the number of games lost to the total number of games played. _____

Solve for the unknown in each proportion.

8. $\dfrac{8}{5} = \dfrac{x}{60}$

9. $\dfrac{7}{2} = \dfrac{140}{c}$

10. $\dfrac{9}{m} = \dfrac{36}{20}$

Use a proportion to solve each problem.

11. A photograph that is 10 inches wide and 12 inches long was reduced to be 4 inches long. Find the width of the reduced photograph.

12. According to interviews, 4 out of 5 people drive to Alicia's exercise class. There are 75 people in the exercise class. How many of them drive to class?

Check your answers on page 201.

Percent Basics

We often read about and hear about percents. The sports pages and business pages of newspapers use percents. Stores use percents. Television news reports include percents.

We use percents when we talk about a part of a whole. *Percent* means "per hundred." A percent always describes part of one hundred.

A city council has 10 members. 100% of the city council is all 10 members.

60% of the city council is 6 members.

50% of the city council is 5 members.

10% of the city council is 1 member.

In this chapter, you will learn how to express percents. You will also learn how to find a percent of a number and to calculate what percent one number is of another.

Talk Math

Do these activities with a partner or a group.

1. Describe situations in which you use percents.
2. Take turns saying a decimal or a fraction and changing it to hundredths. For example, you might say, "One half." Your partner should respond, "50 hundredths."

Hundredths

Fractions divide 1 whole into 2, 3, 4, or more parts. Decimals divide 1 whole into 10 parts, 100 parts, 1,000 parts, and so on. Percents always divide 1 whole into 100 parts. 100 percent always represents 1 whole.

Percent is shown with the sign %. This sign is read as "percent."

> **LANGUAGE Tip**
>
> The word *percent* comes from the word root *cent*, which means "100." Here are some other *cent* words.
>
> | | |
> |---|---|
> | cent | $\frac{1}{100}$ of a dollar |
> | centimeter | $\frac{1}{100}$ of a meter |
> | century | 100 years |

40 percent of each rectangle is shaded.

$\frac{4}{10} = \frac{40}{100} = 40\%$

60 percent of each rectangle is unshaded.

$\frac{6}{10} = \frac{60}{100} = 60\%$

Exercise 1

Write the percent of each shape that is shaded and the percent that is unshaded.

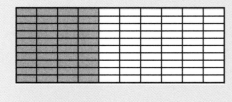

1. **a.** Percent shaded? _____
   b. Percent unshaded? _____

2. **a.** Percent shaded? _____
   b. Percent unshaded? _____

Circle the percent in each sentence. Then write the amount using the % symbol.

3. A computer store is having a 25 percent sale on all printers. _____

4. Waiters hope that diners will leave at least a 15 percent tip. _____

5. Mrs. Anderson has a mortgage that charges 7 percent interest. _____

6. Only 18 percent of all 18-year-olds at a college are registered voters. _____

7. A candy bar with 225 calories is forty-two percent fat. _____

Check your answers on page 201.

Percents as Parts of a Whole

Percents are used to show the parts of a whole amount. A circle graph is an example of percents used in this way. The whole circle represents 100%, or the total amount. Each part of the circle represents a percent, or a part, or the total amount. All the percents must add up to 100%.

> What amount is 100%? What amounts are 40% and 60%?
>
> In a survey of 20 people, 8 people were Democrats, and 12 were Republicans.
>
>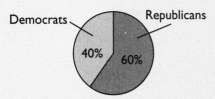
>
> 100% of the survey is 20 people.
>
> 40% of the people were Democrats.
>
> 60% were Republicans.
>
> Notice that 40% and 60% add up to 100%.

Exercise 2

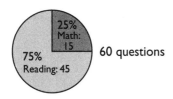

1. a. What is 100%? _____
    b. What is 25%? _____
    c. What is 75%? _____

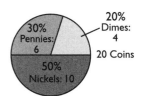

3. a. What is 100%? _____
    b. What is 20%? _____
    c. What is 30%? _____
    d. What is 50%? _____

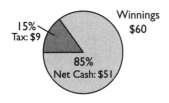

2. a. What is 100%? _____
    b. What is 15%? _____
    c. What is 85%? _____

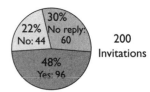

4. a. What is 100%? _____
    b. What is 48%? _____
    c. What is 22%? _____
    d. What is 30%? _____

Check your answers on page 201.

Percent = Decimal = Fraction

A percent, a decimal, and a fraction can all represent the same amount.

Most percents can be changed to decimals without doing any math operation. A percent tells the number of parts out of 100. A two-place decimal also tells the number of parts out of 100.

To change a percent to a decimal, move the decimal point two places to the left, and drop the % sign. (A percent is understood to have a decimal point at the right end.)

Change each percent to a decimal.

$50\% = 0.50 = 0.5$ Move the point in the percent 2 places to the left.

$8\% = 0.08$ Write a 0 to the left of 8% to get 2 places.

$175\% = 1.75$

In the first example, the hundredths place is a zero. It can be dropped. (For a review of dropping end zeros in decimals, reread page 105.)

Exercise 3

Change the percents to decimals, and simplify the answers.

1. $10\% = $ _____
2. $5\% = $ _____
3. $42\% = $ _____
4. $25\% = $ _____
5. $75\% = $ _____
6. $80\% = $ _____
7. $4.5\% = $ _____
8. $300\% = $ _____
9. $120\% = $ _____

Check your answers on page 201.

To change a percent to a fraction, write the percent as a fraction with a denominator of 100. Then reduce the fraction to lowest terms.

Change 50% to a fraction. $50\% = \dfrac{50}{100}$ $\dfrac{50 \div 50}{100 \div 50} = \dfrac{1}{2}$

Exercise 4

Change each percent to a fraction. Reduce all fractions to lowest terms.

1. $10\% = $
2. $5\% = $
3. $42\% = $
4. $25\% = $
5. $75\% = $
6. $80\% = $
7. $30\% = $
8. $95\% = $
9. $125\% = $

Check your answers on page 201.

Finding a Percent of a Number with Decimals

In the most common percent problems, you have to find a percent of a number. The phrase "percent of" tells you that you must multiply to solve the problem. Change the percent to an equivalent decimal or fraction. Then multiply.

Use decimals when you are solving percent problems on a calculator.

> What is 25% of 96?
> 25% = 0.25   Change 25% to a decimal.
> 0.25 × 96 = 24.00 or 24   Multiply 96 by 0.25.
>   25% of 96 is 24.

Exercise 5

First change each percent to a decimal. Then use a calculator to solve the problem.

1. 25% of 80   4. 30% of 200   7. 90% of 450

2. 8% of 240   5. 45% of 120   8. 1.5% of 300

3. 50% of 92   6. 75% of 64   9. 150% of 60

Problems 10–14 are based on the circle graph.

10. How many students are Latinos?
    _____

11. How many students are Africans?
    _____

12. How many students are Eastern Europeans?
    _____

13. How many students are Asians?
    _____

14. How many students are of other ethnic backgrounds? _____

Ethnic Breakdown of Students in ESL class

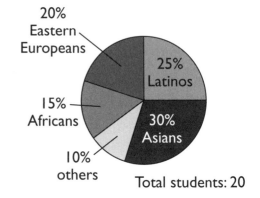

20% Eastern Europeans

25% Latinos

15% Africans

30% Asians

10% others

Total students: 20

Check your answers on page 201.

Finding a Percent of a Number with Fractions

To find a percent of a number, you can change the percent to an equivalent fraction. If you do not have a calculator, this method is sometimes easier than multiplying by a decimal.

What is 30% of 90?

$$30\% = \frac{30}{100} = \frac{3}{10}$$

$$\frac{3}{10} \times 90 = 27$$

Change 30% to a fraction and reduce.

Multiply 90 by $\frac{3}{10}$

30% of 90 is 27.

Exercise 6

Solve each problem. First change each percent to an equivalent fraction.

1. 25% of 60 =

2. 40% of 140 =

3. 10% of 250 =

4. 50% of 82 =

5. 35% of 120 =

6. 75% of 144 =

7. 80% of 250 =

8. 90% of 70 =

9. 150% of 18 =

These problems are based on the circle graph on page 172. To solve, first change each percent to a fraction.

10. How many students are Latinos? _____

11. How many students are Africans? _____

12. How many students are Eastern Europeans? _____

13. How many students are Asians? _____

14. How many students are of other ethnic backgrounds? _____

Check your answers on page 201.

Common Equivalents

Below is a chart with some of the most common percents, along with their decimal and fraction equivalents. Sometimes the fraction equivalent is much easier to work with than the decimal. For example, to find $12\frac{1}{2}\%$ of a number, it is easier to multiply by $\frac{1}{8}$ than to multiply by 0.125.

Take the time to memorize the list.

Percent	Decimal	Fraction		Percent	Decimal	Fraction
25%	0.25	$\frac{1}{4}$		$12\frac{1}{2}\%$	0.125	$\frac{1}{8}$
50%	0.5	$\frac{1}{2}$		$37\frac{1}{2}\%$	0.375	$\frac{3}{8}$
75%	0.75	$\frac{3}{4}$		$62\frac{1}{2}\%$	0.625	$\frac{5}{8}$
				$87\frac{1}{2}\%$	0.875	$\frac{7}{8}$
20%	0.2	$\frac{1}{5}$		10%	0.1	$\frac{1}{10}$
40%	0.4	$\frac{2}{5}$		30%	0.3	$\frac{3}{10}$
60%	0.6	$\frac{3}{5}$		70%	0.7	$\frac{7}{10}$
80%	0.8	$\frac{4}{5}$		90%	0.9	$\frac{9}{10}$
$33\frac{1}{3}\%$	$0.33\frac{1}{3}$	$\frac{1}{3}$		$16\frac{2}{3}\%$	$0.16\frac{2}{3}$	$\frac{1}{6}$
$66\frac{2}{3}\%$	$0.66\frac{2}{3}$	$\frac{2}{3}$		$83\frac{1}{3}\%$	$0.83\frac{1}{3}$	$\frac{5}{6}$

Exercise 7

Solve each problem by using an equivalent decimal or fraction from the table above. In parentheses after each problem is a recommendation for the easier equivalent. If the recommendation says *either*, both equivalents are easy.

1. 40% of 45 (either)

2. $33\frac{1}{3}\%$ of 75 (fraction)

3. $62\frac{1}{2}\%$ of 72 (fraction)

4. 75% of 80 (either)

5. $16\frac{2}{3}\%$ of 120 (fraction)

6. 60% of 150 (either)

7. $66\frac{2}{3}\%$ of 300 (fraction)

8. $37\frac{1}{2}\%$ of 400 (fraction)

9. 50% of 240 (either)

Check your answers on page 202.

Finding a Percent of a Number Word Problems

To find a percent of a number, first change the percent to an equivalent decimal or fraction. Then multiply. (For a review of multiplying decimals, reread pages 112–115. For a review of multiplying fractions, reread pages 149–152.)

> Cheryl works in an office 35 hours a week. She estimates that she spends 20% of her time typing. How many hours does she type in a week?
>
> **a.** decimal problem
> $20\% = 0.2$ Change 20% to a decimal.
> $0.2 \times 35 = 7.0 = 7$ Multiply 35 by 0.2. Cheryl types 7 hours a week.
>
> **b.** fraction problem
> $20\% = \dfrac{20}{100} = \dfrac{1}{5}$ Change 20% to a fraction.
> $\dfrac{1}{5} \times \dfrac{35}{1} = \dfrac{7}{1} = 7$ Multiply 35 by $\dfrac{1}{5}$ Cheryl types 7 hours a week.

Exercise 8

For each problem, use both a decimal and a fraction to solve the problem.

1. A job exam has 120 questions. To qualify, you need to score at least 70%. How many questions do you need to answer correctly?
    a. decimal problem   **b.** fraction problem

2. Tom's restaurant bill is $28. For a 15% tip, how much should Tom leave?
    a. decimal problem   **b.** fraction problem

3. A shoe store sells a pair of shoes for $85. A mail-order house sells the same pair of shoes at 80% of that price. How much do the shoes cost by mail order?
    a. decimal problem   **b.** fraction problem

4. Anna plans to borrow $2,500 from a bank. The bank charges 10% interest. How much will she pay in interest?
    a. decimal problem   **b.** fraction problem

5. A doctor told her patient to reduce her calorie intake by 30%. If the patient usually eats 2,800 calories a day, how many calories should she cut out?
    a. decimal problem   **b.** fraction problem

Check your answers on page 202.

Two-Step Percent Problems

In real life, a percent of a number is often added to or subtracted from an original amount. Think about the next example carefully.

> This year Maria pays $600 a month for rent. Next year her rent goes up 5%. How much will her monthly rent be next year?
>
> | | |
> |---|---|
> | 5% = 0.05 | Change 5% to a decimal or a fraction. |
> | 0.05 × $600 = $30 | Find 5% of $600 (the increase). |
> | $600 + $30 = $630 | Add the increase to her old rent. |
> | | Maria's new rent will be $630 a month. |

Exercise 9

1. A laptop computer originally sold for $590. Now it is on sale for 15% less. Find the sale price.

2. Lucy now earns $610 a week. Her supervisor is giving her a 6% raise. How much will she make then?

3. Phil and his daughter ate lunch at their favorite coffee shop. The bill was $18.40. If Phil leaves a 15% tip, what is the total cost of the lunch including the tip?

4. Sam used to weigh 196 pounds. He went on a diet and lost 10% of his weight. What was his new weight?

5. Mr. and Mrs. Garcia paid $145,000 for their house. They sold their house eight years later for 30% more. What was the sale price of the house?

6. A jacket is on sale for $89. Find the total cost of the jacket including 6% sales tax.

7. Pete bought a used car for $3,500. He made a down payment of 20% of the price and borrowed the rest. How much did he borrow?

8. Joan has to pay 12% interest on her $2,000 student loan. How much does she have to pay including interest?

Check your answers on page 202.

Finding What Percent One Number Is of Another

To find what percent one number is of another, first make a fraction. (The number following *of* is usually the denominator.) Then change the fraction to a percent.

To change a fraction to a percent, multiply the fraction by 100%.

> 21 is what percent of 35?
> $$\frac{21}{35} = \frac{3}{5}$$
> 21 is the numerator, and 35 is the denominator.
> Reduce the fraction.
>
> $$\frac{3}{5} \times 100\% = 60\%$$
> Change the fraction to a percent.
> 21 is 60% of 35.

Exercise 10

1. 15 is what percent of 30?

2. What percent of 240 is 24?

3. What percent of 54 is 18?

4. 28 is what percent of 35?

5. What percent of 72 is 12?

6. 8 is what percent of 200?

7. What percent of 64 is 16?

8. 45 is what percent of 75?

9. What percent of 80 is 60?

10. 90 is what percent of 720?

11. On a test with 20 questions, Boris got 18 questions right. What percent of the questions did he get right?

12. Together Mark and Jane bring home $2,800 a month. They pay $700 each month for rent. Rent uses what percent of their take-home pay?

13. There are 30 students in Mrs. Brown's government class. 12 of the students are men. Men make up what percent of the class?

Check your answers on page 202.

Percent Checkup

1. Change each percent to a decimal.

   a. 60% = _____   **b.** 12% = _____   **c.** 3% = _____

2. Change each percent to a fraction.

   a. 15% = _____   **b.** 40% = _____   **c.** 4% = _____

Questions 3–7 are based on the circle graph.

3. What is 100% of the budget?

4. How much is the monthly rent?

5. How much goes for food each month?

6. How much money is spent on bills each month?

7. How much money is saved each month?

8. Use a decimal to find 35% of 400.

9. Use a fraction to find $33\frac{1}{3}$% of 810.

10. Of the 24 students in Mr. Saba's computer class, 18 are women. What percent of the class is women?

Check your answers on page 202.

Points to Remember

- A percent is a part of a whole. 100% represents the whole amount.

- To change a percent to a decimal, move the decimal point in the percent two places to the left. Then drop the % sign.

- To change a percent to a fraction, write the percent as the numerator and 100 as the denominator. Then drop the % sign.

- To find a percent of a number, first change each percent to an equivalent decimal or fraction. Then multiply.

Posttest

Check your understanding of the skills that you learned in this book.

PART A

1. Write three thousand, five hundred nine in digits. _____

2. Write fourteen thousand, two hundred in digits. _____

3. In 5,687, which digit is in the hundreds place? _____

4. Round 2,419 to the nearest hundred. _____

5. Round 758 to the nearest ten. _____

6. In $42.16, which digit is in the tens place? _____

7. In $80.53, which digit is in the dimes, or tenths, place? _____

8. Round $12.82 to the nearest dollar. _____

9. Round $8.74 to the nearest dime. _____

10. In the number 73.406, which digit is in the tenths place? _____

11. In the number 125.68, which digit is in the hundredths place? _____

12. Use digits to write four and twelve thousandths as a decimal. _____

13. Use digits to write eleven and eight hundredths as a decimal. _____

14. Round 0.639 to the nearest tenth. _____

15. Round 25.418 to the nearest hundredth. _____

16. Round $7 \frac{3}{8}$ to the nearest whole number. _____

17. Round $12 \frac{5}{6}$ to the nearest whole number. _____

18. Reduce $\frac{14}{35}$ to lowest terms. _____

19. Reduce $\frac{18}{24}$ to lowest terms. _____

20. Change $\frac{14}{4}$ to a mixed number and reduce. _____

21. Change 0.45 to a fraction and reduce. _____

22. A class has 15 women and 9 men. Write and simplify the ratio of women to men. _____

23. Jan got 8 problems right and 2 wrong on a test. Write and simplify the ratio of the number of problems right to the total number of problems. _____

24. Elena drove 58 miles on 2 gallons of gasoline. Find her gas usage in miles per gallon. _____

25. In the circle graph, what amount does 100% represent? _____

26. In the circle graph, what amount does 35% represent? _____

27. Change 18% to a decimal. _____

28. Change 7.5% to a decimal. _____

29. Change 65% to a fraction and reduce. _____

30. Change 32% to a fraction and reduce. _____

Los Altos: Population 200

21% Children: 42

44% Adults: 88

35% Elderly: 70

Posttest

PART B

Unit 1: Whole Numbers

1. $38 + 79 =$

2. $72 - 15 =$

3. $2 \times 235 =$

4. $12 \times 44 =$

5. $378 \div 9 =$

6. $156 \div 12 =$

Unit 2: Money

7. $\$156 + \$289 =$

8. $\$13.14 - \$11.99 =$

9. $\$5 - \$1.85 =$

10. $12 \times \$4.25 =$

11. $\$21 \div 4 =$

12. $\$3.05 \div 5 =$

Unit 3: Decimals

Simplify each answer.

13. $0.8 + 2.45 + 1.076 =$

14. $3 - 2.5 =$

15. $4 \times 4.36 =$

16. $0.5 \times 2.3 =$

17. $1.2 \times 4.15 =$

18. $1.3 \div 2 =$

19. $0.75 \div 5 =$

20. $4.6 \div 0.2 =$

21. $24.6 \div 1.2 =$

Unit 4: Fractions

In the answers, change improper fractions to mixed numbers. Reduce fractions.

22. $\frac{1}{4} + \frac{2}{3} =$

23. $2\frac{1}{2} + 1\frac{3}{4} =$

24. $\frac{3}{4} - \frac{1}{2} =$

25. $3\frac{1}{3} - 1\frac{1}{2} =$

26. $2\frac{3}{4} \times 4 =$

27. $\frac{3}{5} \times 2\frac{1}{2} =$

28. $\frac{3}{4} \div \frac{1}{2} =$

29. $3\frac{1}{2} \div 2 =$

30. $6\frac{1}{4} \div 2\frac{1}{2} =$

Unit 5: Ratio and Percent

31. Simplify the ratio $24 : 30$.

32. Solve for the unknown in $\frac{2}{3} = \frac{x}{9}$.

33. Solve for the unknown in $\frac{9}{c} = \frac{15}{20}$.

34. What is 8% of 240?

35. Find 15% of 60.

36. 21 is what percent of 84?

PART C

The following questions are based on the airline advertisement. Show your work.

One-way fares from **San Francisco** to **Chicago**	
☆ Airline A	$284
☆ Airline B	$373

1. How much less is the fare on Airline A than on Airline B?

2. How much is a round-trip ticket from Airline A?

3. Airline A gives a 10% discount to senior citizens. How much is taken off the fare?

4. Airline B gives a 20% discount for buying a ticket 60 days in advance. What is the price of a ticket on Airline B if it is purchased 60 days in advance?

PART D

The following questions are based on the grocery ad. First estimate each answer. Then use a calculator to find the exact answers.

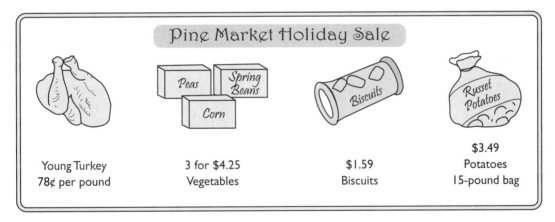

Pine Market Holiday Sale

Young Turkey 78¢ per pound

3 for $4.25 Vegetables

$1.59 Biscuits

$3.49 Potatoes 15-pound bag

1. What is the cost of a 10-pound turkey?

2. At the sale price, what is the price for 1 pound of potatoes?

3. At the sales price, how much does 1 package of vegetables cost?

4. If a shopper uses a 25¢-off coupon for the biscuits, how much do the biscuits cost?

5. A shopper bought 1 bag of potatoes, 3 boxes of peas, 1 can of biscuits, and 1 turkey that cost $9.36. Find the total cost of the purchases.

6. If the shopper in the last problem paid with $20, how much change did she get?

PART E

Questions 1–5 are based on the recipe.

BANANA BREAD   Yield: 2 loaves

Ingredients

$1\frac{3}{4}$ cups white flour

$\frac{3}{4}$ cup whole wheat flour

$\frac{1}{4}$ cup oat flour

$\frac{1}{2}$ tsp salt

2 tsp. baking soda

1 cup liquid shortening

$1\frac{3}{4}$ cups sugar

3 eggs, slightly beaten

2 cups mashed bananas

1 cup chopped nuts

$\frac{1}{2}$ cup raisins

1. How many total cups of flour are used for the recipe?

2. How much more white flour is used than oat flour?

3. If you double the recipe, how much oat flour will you need?

4. If you make only half of the recipe, how much sugar will you need?

5. The ratio of cups of bananas to one full recipe is 2 to 1. How many cups of mashed bananas would you need to make the recipe three times?

PART F

The following questions are about this advertisement. Round each answer to the nearest penny.

1. What are the savings on the dishes?

2. What is the cost of 2 sets of dishes?

SALE!   SALE!
Festive Floral Dishes
Sale: $59.99
20-piece set
$80, regular price

3. The set has 4 settings. What is the cost per setting?

4. Gloria plans to buy 1 set of Festive Floral while the dishes are on sale. If the sales tax in her state is 6%, how much will be added to the sales price?

5. Including the 6% sales tax, what will be the total cost for 1 set of dishes?

Check your answers on pages 183–184.

Posttest Answer Key

PART A, page 179

1. 3,509
2. 14,200
3. 6
4. 2,400
5. 760
6. 4
7. 5
8. $13.00 or $13
9. $8.70
10. 4
11. 8
12. 4.012
13. 11.08
14. 0.6
15. 25.42
16. 7
17. 13
18. $\frac{2}{5}$
19. $\frac{3}{4}$
20. $3\frac{2}{4} = 3\frac{1}{2}$
21. $\frac{45}{100} = \frac{9}{20}$
22. $15 : 9 = 5 : 3$
23. $8 : 10 = 4 : 5$
24. 29 miles per gallon
25. 200 people
26. 70 elderly people
27. 0.18
28. 0.075
29. $\frac{65}{100} = \frac{13}{20}$
30. $\frac{32}{100} = \frac{8}{25}$

PART B, page 180

1. 117
2. 57
3. 470
4. 528
5. 42
6. 13
7. $445
8. $1.15
9. $3.15
10. $51.00
11. $5.25
12. $.61
13. 4.326
14. 0.5
15. 17.44
16. 1.15
17. 4.98
18. 0.65
19. 0.15
20. 23
21. 20.5
22. $\frac{11}{12}$
23. $4\frac{1}{4}$
24. $\frac{1}{4}$
25. $1\frac{5}{6}$
26. 11
27. $1\frac{1}{2}$
28. $1\frac{1}{2}$
29. $1\frac{3}{4}$
30. $2\frac{1}{2}$
31. $4 : 5$
32. $x = 6$
33. $c = 12$
34. 19.2
35. 9
36. 25%

PART C, page 181

1. $373 − $284 = $89
2. 2 × $284 = $568
3. 0.1 × $284 = $28.40 *or* 1/10 × $284 = $28.40
4. 0.2 × $373 = $74.60; $373 − $74.60 = $298.40

PART D, page 181

Estimates may vary.

1. Estimate: 10 × $0.80 = $8   Exact: $7.80
2. Estimate: $3 ÷ 15 = $0.20   Exact: $0.23 to nearest penny
3. Estimate: $4.50 ÷ 3 = $1.50   Exact: $1.42 to nearest penny
4. Estimate: $1.60 − $0.25 = $1.35   Exact: $1.34
5. Estimate: $3 + $4 + $2 + $9 = $18   Exact: $18.69
6. Estimate: $20 − $19 = $1   Exact: $1.31

PART E, page 182

1. $1\frac{3}{4} + \frac{3}{4} + \frac{1}{4} = 2\frac{3}{4}$ cups

2. $1\frac{3}{4} - \frac{1}{4} = 1\frac{2}{4} = 1\frac{1}{2}$ cups

3. $2 \times \frac{1}{4} = \frac{2}{4} = \frac{1}{2}$ cup

4. $1\frac{3}{4} \times \frac{1}{2} = \frac{7}{8}$ cup

5. $\frac{2}{1} = \frac{x}{3}$; $x = 6$ cups

PART F, page 182

1. $\$80 - \$59.99 = \$20.01$

2. $2 \times \$59.99 = \$119.98$

3. $\$59.99 \div 4 = \$15.00$

4. $0.06 \times \$59.99 = \$3.60$

5. $\$59.99 + \$3.60 = \$63.59$

Posttest Evaluation Chart

Use the answer key on pages 183–184 to check your answers to the Posttest. On the chart below, circle the item number of each question you missed. Then write the number of correct answers you had for each skill. If you need practice in any skill, refer to the chapter that covers that skill.

	Chapter	Skill	Item Numbers	Number Correct
Part A	1	Whole Numbers	1, 2, 3, 4, 5	
	8	Money	6, 7, 8, 9	
	10	Decimals	10, 11, 12, 13, 14, 15	
	12, 13	Fractions	16, 17, 18, 19, 20, 21	
	15	Ratio	22, 23, 24	
	16	Percent	25, 26, 27, 28, 29, 30	
Part B	3	Addition	1	
	4	Subtraction	2	
	6	Multiplication	3, 4	
	7	Division	5, 6	
	9	Money	7, 8, 9, 10, 11, 12	
	11	Decimals	13, 14, 15, 16, 17, 18, 19, 20, 21	
	14	Fractions	22, 23, 24, 25, 26, 27, 28, 29, 30	
	15	Ratio	31, 32, 33	
	16	Percent	34, 35, 36	
Part C	9	Money	1, 2	
	16	Percent	3, 4	
Part D	9	Money	1, 2, 3, 4, 5, 6	
Part E	14	Fractions	1, 2, 3, 4	
	15	Ratio	5	
Part F	9	Money	1, 2, 3	
	16	Percent	4, 5	

Answer Key

Unit 1: Whole Numbers

Chapter 1: Whole Number Basics

Exercise 1, page 3

1. 4	5. 6	9. b. 2,766
2. 7	6. 2,000	10. d. 184
3. 80	7. 90	
4. 100	8. c. 2,927	

Exercise 2, page 4

1. hundreds tens		4. 900
2. hundreds ones		5. 3,000
3. tens ones		6. 90

Exercise 3, page 5

1. tens	8. ten thousands
2. ones	9. 4,000
3. hundreds	10. 100,000
4. hundreds ones	11. 8,000
5. hundreds tens	12. millions
6. thousands ones	13. 9
7. 4	14. 70,000

Exercise 4, pages 6–7

1. thousand hundred
2. thousand
3. thousand hundred
4. thousand
5. thousand hundred
6. million thousand
7. million thousand
8. million thousand hundred

9. 305	14. 8,015
10. 420	15. 15,150
11. 912	16. 170,000
12. 2,100	17. 304,912
13. 3,406	18. 5,300,000

19. 7,010,425
20. four hundred thirty-six
21. five hundred eight
22. one thousand, seven hundred forty
23. six thousand, fourteen
24. twelve thousand, three hundred
25. thirty-five thousand, two hundred ten
26. sixty-five thousand, three hundred
27. one hundred thousand, fifty-four
28. four hundred twenty thousand
29. eight million, six hundred thousand
30. three million, four hundred nineteen thousand

Exercise 5, page 9

1. 30	11. 200	21. 2,000
2. 30	12. 200	22. 3,000
3. 70	13. 500	23. 4,000
4. 120	14. 2,300	24. 8,000
5. 160	15. 4,800	25. 11,000
6. 530	16. 5,100	26. 14,000
7. 810	17. 10,100	27. 57,000
8. 2,310	18. 22,800	28. 102,000
9. 3,260	19. 88,600	29. 423,000
10. 10,430	20. 131,500	30. 688,000

Exercise 6, page 10

Answers will vary depending on calculator.
1. The display shows the digit 0.
2. 8 digits
3. The display shows the digit 0.

Whole Number Basics Checkup, page 12

1. 3	2. 800	3. 3	4. 6,000

5. thousand hundred
6. thousand hundred

7. 1,230	8. 28,750	9. 730,140

10. eight hundred sixty
11. nine thousand, five hundred three
12. fourteen thousand, ninety

13. 630	15. 43,000	17. 3, 5, 8
14. 800	16. 510,000	

Chapter 2: Addition and Subtraction Facts

Exercise 1, page 14

1. 1	4. 0	7. 0	10. 0
2. 0	5. 3	8. 4	
3. 2	6. 1	9. 1	

Exercise 2, page 14

1. 5	6. 2	11. 2	16. 2
2. 2	7. 1	12. 1	17. 1
3. 1	8. 0	13. 0	18. 0
4. 0	9. 7	14. 8	
5. 6	10. 3	15. 3	

Answer Key

Exercise 3, page 15

1. 9	7. 4	13. 3	19. 5
2. 4	8. 3	14. 2	20. 4
3. 3	9. 2	15. 5	21. 6
4. 2	10. 1	16. 4	22. 5
5. 1	11. 5	17. 3	
6. 0	12. 4	18. 6	

Exercise 4, page 15

1. 7	2. 6	3. 7	4. 8

Exercise 5, page 17

1. 9	11. 9	21. 9	31. 9
2. 8	12. 8	22. 8	32. 8
3. 7	13. 7	23. 7	33. 7
4. 6	14. 6	24. 6	34. 6
5. 5	15. 5	25. 5	35. 5
6. 4	16. 4	26. 4	36. 4
7. 3	17. 3	27. 3	37. 3
8. 2	18. 2	28. 2	38. 2
9. 1	19. 1	29. 1	39. 1
10. 0	20. 0	30. 0	40. 0

Exercise 6, page 17

1. 9	14. 6	27. 3	40. 0
2. 8	15. 5	28. 2	41. 9
3. 7	16. 4	29. 1	42. 8
4. 6	17. 3	30. 0	43. 7
5. 5	18. 2	31. 9	44. 6
6. 4	19. 1	32. 8	45. 5
7. 3	20. 0	33. 7	46. 4
8. 2	21. 9	34. 6	47. 3
9. 1	22. 8	35. 5	48. 2
10. 0	23. 7	36. 4	49. 1
11. 9	24. 6	37. 3	50. 0
12. 8	25. 5	38. 2	
13. 7	26. 4	39. 1	

Addition and Subtraction Facts Checkup, page 18

1. 5	9. 18	17. 14	25. 5
2. 7	10. 15	18. 10	26. 3
3. 3	11. 15	19. 8	27. 6
4. 8	12. 14	20. 15	28. 1
5. 10	13. 9	21. 16	29. 5
6. 13	14. 10	22. 9	30. 4
7. 12	15. 12	23. 17	31. 4
8. 11	16. 12	24. 11	32. 9

33. 8	37. 3	41. 9	45. 9
34. 9	38. 3	42. 4	46. 6
35. 8	39. 5	43. 6	47. 7
36. 7	40. 8	44. 4	48. 8

Chapter 3: Addition

Exercise 1, page 20

Numbers in Exercise 1 can be in either order.

1. 35 + 18 =	6. 437 + 8 =
2. 44 + 20 =	7. 96 + 3 =
3. 161 + 465 =	8. 49 + 207 =
4. 230 + 304 =	9. 153 + 68 =
5. 255 + 99 =	10. 75 + 411 =

Exercise 2, page 21

1. 29	2. 467	3. 47	4. 385

Exercise 3, page 21

1. 557	2. 968	3. 1,798	4. 2,398

Exercise 4, page 22

1. 42	3. 70	5. 893	7. 749
2. 45	4. 396	6. 899	8. 898

Exercise 5, page 23

1. 42	4. 84	7. 496
2. 30	5. 95	8. 383
3. 62	6. 221	9. 273

Exercise 6, page 24

1. 127	4. 846	7. 314	10. 340
2. 808	5. 143	8. 589	11. 605
3. 341	6. 140	9. 730	12. 403

Exercise 7, page 25

1. 109	4. 872	7. 110
2. 171	5. 695	8. 660
3. 570	6. 1,154	9. 1,052

Exercise 8, page 26

1. Exact: 49   Est.: 10 + 30 + 10 = 50
2. Exact: 114 Est.: 0 + 20 + 90 = 110
3. Exact: 325 Est.: 90 + 100 + 100 = 290
4. Exact: 96   Est.: 50 + 10 + 40 = 100
5. Exact: 526 Est.: 50 + 50 + 400 = 500
6. Exact: 876 Est.: 300 + 300 + 300 = 900
7. Exact: 778 Est.: 200 + 400 + 200 = 800
8. Exact: 1,309
    Est.: 300 + 80 + 900 = 1,280

9. Exact: 993 Est.: 50 + 600 + 400
                    = 1,050
10. Exact: 104 Est.: 10 + 40 + 30 + 20
                    = 100
11. Exact: 133 Est.: 50 + 20 + 30 + 40
                    = 140
12. Exact: 342 Est.: 100 + 80 + 20 + 100
                    = 300

Exercise 9, page 27

1. Estimate: 8,000 + 800 = 8,800
   Exact: 9,084 people
2. Estimate: 300 + 100 = 400
   Exact: 391 miles
3. Estimate: $700 + $40 = $740
   Exact: $736
4. Estimate: 2,000 + 500 = 2,500
   Exact: 2,344 seats
5. Estimate; you cannot determine exactly how much paint you will use.
6. Estimate; how much each person will eat can vary, so you will not know exactly how much cake you need.
7. Exact; you must charge the exact price.
8. Estimate; you cannot tell exactly how much gas you need.
9. Exact; you need the exact amount in your account before you write a check.

Addition Checkup, page 28

1. 69   2. 989   3. 1,258   4. 1,852
5. Exact: 747   Est.: 300 + 70 + 400 = 770
6. Exact: 1,078
   Est.: 100 + 600 + 400 = 1,100
7. Exact: 2,438
   Est.: 500 + 1,000 + 700 = 2,200
8. Exact: 506 miles
   Estimate: 200 + 300 = 500
9. Exact: $1,184
   Estimate: $400 + $100 + $600 = $1,100
10. Estimate; you cannot tell exactly how long the trip will take.

Chapter 4: Subtraction

Exercise 1, page 30

1. 7	4. 60	7. 24	10. 24
2. 24	5. 123	8. 321	11. 206
3. 32	6. 120	9. 550	12. 362

Exercise 2, page 31

1. 411	3. 314	5. 1,031
2. 307	4. 623	6. 753

Exercise 3, page 32

1. 8	4. 29	7. 64	10. 29
2. 16	5. 47	8. 47	11. 45
3. 9	6. 9	9. 19	12. 78

Exercise 4, page 33

1. 58	3. 183	5. 39	7. 635
2. 63	4. 216	6. 177	8. 208

Exercise 5, page 34

1. 21	3. 40	5. 148	7. 652
2. 26	4. 237	6. 477	8. 230

Exercise 6, page 35

1. Exact: 62   Estimate: 80 − 20 = 60
2. Exact: 45   Estimate: 50 − 10 = 40
3. Exact: 7   Estimate: 60 − 50 = 10
4. Exact: 44   Estimate: 90 − 50 = 40
5. Exact: 260   Estimate: 300 − 20 = 280
6. Exact: 457   Estimate: 900 − 400 = 500
7. Exact: 381   Estimate: 400 − 30 = 370
8. Exact: 108   Estimate: 300 − 200 = 100
9. Exact: 616   Estimate: 800 − 200 = 600
10. Exact: 299   Estimate: 500 − 200 = 300
11. Exact: 529   Estimate: 800 − 300 = 500
12. Exact: 207   Estimate: 900 − 700 = 200
13. Exact: 748   Estimate: 800 − 60 = 740
14. Exact: 346   Estimate: 600 − 300 = 300
15. Exact: 506   Estimate: 700 − 200 = 500

Answer Key

Exercise 7, page 37

1. Estimate: 60 – 30 = 30
   Exact: 25 miles per hour
2. Estimate: 60 + 30 = 90
   Exact: 87 miles
3. Estimate: $80 – $60 = $20
   Exact: $17
4. Estimate: 30 – 20 = 10
   Exact: 9 vacation days
5. Estimate: $500 – $80 = $420
   Exact: $415
6. Estimate: 600 + 900 = 1,500.
   Then 2,400 – 1,500 = 900
   Exact: 920 calories

Subtraction Checkup, page 38

1. 45   3. 510   5. 235
2. 424   4. 127   6. 177
7. Exact: 85   Est.: 600 – 500 = 100
8. Exact: 335   Est.: 700 – 400 = 300
9. Exact: 618   Est.: 900 – 300 = 600
10. $125   11. $533   12. 167 pounds

Chapter 5: Multiplication and Division Facts

Exercise 1, page 40

1. 1	10. 2	19. 3	28. 4
2. 2	11. 4	20. 6	29. 8
3. 3	12. 6	21. 9	30. 12
4. 4	13. 8	22. 12	31. 16
5. 5	14. 10	23. 15	32. 20
6. 6	15. 12	24. 18	33. 24
7. 7	16. 14	25. 21	34. 28
8. 8	17. 16	26. 24	35. 32
9. 9	18. 18	27. 27	36. 36

Exercise 2, page 41

1. 5	11. 14	21. 48
2. 10	12. 21	22. 56
3. 15	13. 28	23. 9
4. 20	14. 35	24. 18
5. 6	15. 42	25. 27
6. 12	16. 8	26. 36
7. 18	17. 16	27. 45
8. 24	18. 24	28. 54
9. 30	19. 32	29. 63
10. 7	20. 40	30. 72

Exercise 3, page 43

1. 9	10. 9	19. 9	28. 9
2. 8	11. 8	20. 8	29. 8
3. 7	12. 7	21. 7	30. 7
4. 6	13. 6	22. 6	31. 6
5. 5	14. 5	23. 5	32. 5
6. 4	15. 4	24. 4	33. 4
7. 3	16. 3	25. 3	34. 3
8. 2	17. 2	26. 2	35. 2
9. 1	18. 1	27. 1	36. 1

Exercise 4, page 43

1. 9	13. 6	25. 3	37. 9
2. 8	14. 5	26. 2	38. 8
3. 7	15. 4	27. 1	39. 7
4. 6	16. 3	28. 9	40. 6
5. 5	17. 2	29. 8	41. 5
6. 4	18. 1	30. 7	42. 4
7. 3	19. 9	31. 6	43. 3
8. 2	20. 8	32. 5	44. 2
9. 1	21. 7	33. 4	45. 1
10. 9	22. 6	34. 3	
11. 8	23. 5	35. 2	
12. 7	24. 4	36. 1	

Multiplication and Division Facts Checkup, page 44

1. 9	13. 35	25. 6	37. 6
2. 5	14. 36	26. 9	38. 9
3. 18	15. 30	27. 9	39. 8
4. 18	16. 63	28. 5	40. 5
5. 27	17. 64	29. 8	41. 6
6. 40	18. 54	30. 8	42. 1
7. 63	19. 28	31. 7	43. 9
8. 81	20. 25	32. 8	44. 8
9. 56	21. 48	33. 6	45. 7
10. 10	22. 21	34. 8	46. 9
11. 32	23. 49	35. 6	47. 9
12. 24	24. 72	36. 7	48. 6

Chapter 6: Multiplication

Exercise 1, page 47

1. 69	4. 129	7. 216
2. 82	5. 128	8. 128
3. 48	6. 549	9. 355

Exercise 2, page 47

1. 1,248
2. 3,555
3. 2,088
4. 2,736
5. 826
6. 4,055

Exercise 3, page 48

1. 80
2. 90
3. 630
4. 880
5. 2,103
6. 800
7. 4,860
8. 2,008

Exercise 4, page 49

1. 54
2. 180
3. 87
4. 252
5. 576
6. 276
7. 171
8. 340

Exercise 5, page 50

1. 236
2. 3,306
3. 1,112
4. 3,136
5. 416
6. 5,436
7. 1,227
8. 4,842

Exercise 6, page 51

1. 288
2. 416
3. 165
4. 504
5. 396
6. 1,008

Exercise 7, page 52

1. 864
2. 2,835
3. 3,910
4. 4,292
5. 6,882
6. 2,183
7. 4,704
8. 1,482
9. 7,524
10. 47,965
11. 4,301
12. 24,288
13. 59,057
14. 78,200
15. 26,424
16. 44,767

Exercise 8, page 53

1. 150
2. 280
3. 3,650
4. 1,400
5. 900
6. 3,100
7. 7,800
8. 23,900
9. 58,000
10. 70,000
11. 94,000
12. 645,000

Exercise 9, page 54

1. 2,160
2. 7,680
3. 4,100
4. 4,200
5. 5,700
6. 69,400
7. 666,000
8. 240,000

Exercise 10, page 55

1. Estimate: $40 \times 4 = 160$ Exact: 172
2. Estimate: $40 \times 6 = 240$ Exact: 234
3. Estimate: $9 \times 90 = 810$ Exact: 765
4. Estimate: $60 \times 7 = 420$ Exact: 392
5. Estimate: $3 \times 100 = 300$ Exact: 336
6. Estimate: $200 \times 2 = 400$ Exact: 416
7. Estimate: $200 \times 4 = 800$ Exact: 740
8. Estimate: $5 \times 300 = 1,500$ Exact: 1,630

Exercise 11, page 55

1. Estimate: $20 \times 50 = 1,000$ Exact: 810
2. Estimate: $10 \times 70 = 700$ Exact: 1,008
3. Estimate: $30 \times 20 = 600$ Exact: 513
4. Estimate: $40 \times 20 = 800$ Exact: 864
5. Estimate: $60 \times 80 = 4,800$ Exact: 4,592
6. Estimate: $70 \times 40 = 2,800$ Exact: 2,592
7. Est.: $300 \times 70 = 21,000$ Exact: 19,652
8. Estimate: $20 \times 400 = 8,000$ Exact: 9,016

Exercise 12, page 57

1. Est.: $9 \times \$400 = \$3,600$
   Exact: $3,825
2. Est.: $4 \times 30 = 120$
   Exact: 112 protein calories
3. Est.: $100 + 300 = \$400$ Exact: $376
4. Est.: $12 \times \$400 = \$4,800$ Exact: $4,512
5. Est.: $2 \times 40 = 80$ and $5 \times 80 = 400$
   Exact: 380 miles
6. Est.: $10 \times 30 = 300$
   Exact: 377 miles

Multiplication Checkup, page 58

1. 4,254
2. 2,456
3. 4,527
4. 730
5. 3,600
6. 18,000
7. Est.: $60 \times 90 = 5,400$ Exact: 5,244
8. Est.: $80 \times 30 = 2,400$ Exact: 2,324
9. Est.: $300 \times 50 = 15,000$ Exact: 15,288
10. $192
11. 444 pounds
12. $54 \times 35 = 1,890$ words
    No, he will not be able to type 2,000 words in 35 minutes.

Chapter 7: Division

Exercise 1, page 60

1. $48 \div 2$ $2\overline{)48}$
2. $39 \div 6$ $6\overline{)39}$
3. $290 \div 5$ $5\overline{)290}$
4. $248 \div 8$ $8\overline{)248}$
5. $380 \div 10$ $10\overline{)380}$
6. $96 \div 32$ $32\overline{)96}$

Answer Key

Exercise 2, page 61

1.
```
      4 8
  2 )9 6
    - 8
      1 6
    - 1 6
        0
```

3.
```
      1 3
  6 )7 8
    - 6
      1 8
    - 1 8
        0
```

5.
```
      4 1
  2 )8 2
    - 8
      0 2
      - 2
        0
```

2.
```
      1 8
  3 )5 4
    - 3
      2 4
    - 2 4
        0
```

4.
```
      2 3
  4 )9 2
    - 8
      1 2
    - 1 2
        0
```

6.
```
      1 4
  7 )9 8
    - 7
      2 8
    - 2 8
        0
```

Exercise 3, page 62

1.
```
      1 9
  5 )9 5
    - 5
      4 5
    - 4 5
        0
```

3.
```
      1 3
  7 )9 1
    - 7
      2 1
    - 2 1
        0
```

5.
```
      2 3
  4 )9 2
    - 8
      1 2
    - 1 2
        0
```

2.
```
      2 7
  3 )8 1
    - 6
      2 1
    - 2 1
        0
```

4.
```
      1 4
  6 )8 4
    - 6
      2 4
    - 2 4
        0
```

6.
```
      4 9
  2 )9 8
    - 8
      1 8
    - 1 8
        0
```

Exercise 4, page 63

1. 27 r 2
2. 13 r 4
3. 19 r 2
4. 12 r 3
5. 13 r 4
6. 32 r 2
7. 17 r 2
8. 13 r 2
9. 12 r 4

Exercise 5, page 64

1. 127
2. 216
3. 256
4. 117
5. 129
6. 216 r 1
7. 156 r 4
8. 142 r 2
9. 155 r 5

Exercise 6, page 65

1. 83
2. 54
3. 42
4. 59
5. 68 r 2
6. 93 r 3
7. 87 r 1
8. 53 r 4
9. 61 r 2

Exercise 7, page 66

1. 302
2. 160
3. 50 r 5
4. 120
5. 70 r 5
6. 130 r 3

Exercise 8, page 67

1. 4
2. 7
3. 8
4. 6
5. 5
6. 3 r 4
7. 7 r 30
8. 6 r 22
9. 8 r 12

Exercise 9, page 68

1. 18
2. 72
3. 23
4. 41
5. 77
6. 20
7. 13
8. 32
9. 47

Exercise 10, page 69

Estimates will vary.

1. Estimate: $36 \div 6 = 6$ Exact: 6 r 1
2. Estimate: $49 \div 7 = 7$ Exact: 7 r 1
3. Estimate: $63 \div 9 = 7$ Exact: 7 r 2
4. Estimate: $64 \div 8 = 8$ Exact: 8 r 3
5. Estimate: $27 \div 3 = 9$ Exact: 9 r 1
6. Estimate: $45 \div 5 = 9$ Exact: 9 r 3
7. Estimate: $72 \div 9 = 8$ Exact: 7 r 8
8. Estimate: $32 \div 4 = 8$ Exact: 7 r 3
9. Estimate: $56 \div 8 = 7$ Exact: 6 r 7
10. Estimate: $49 \div 7 = 7$ Exact: 7 r 2

Exercise 11, page 70

Estimates will vary.

1. Estimate: $240 \div 6 = 40$ Exact: 43
2. Estimate: $320 \div 8 = 40$ Exact: 39 r 5
3. Estimate: $150 \div 5 = 30$ Exact: 32 r 3
4. Estimate: $210 \div 3 = 70$ Exact: 69
5. Estimate: $450 \div 9 = 50$ Exact: 52
6. Estimate: $350 \div 7 = 50$ Exact: 48
7. Estimate: $400 \div 8 = 50$ Exact: 53 r 1
8. Estimate: $480 \div 6 = 80$ Exact: 78 r 3
9. Estimate: $630 \div 9 = 70$ Exact: 68

Exercise 12, page 71

Estimates will vary.

1. Estimate: $1,600 \div 40 = 40$ Exact: 42
2. Estimate: $3,000 \div 50 = 60$ Exact: 57
3. Estimate: $2,000 \div 20 = 100$
   Exact: 82 r 20
4. Estimate: $1,000 \div 20 = 50$ Exact: 60 r 3
5. Estimate: $3,200 \div 40 = 80$ Exact: 82
6. Estimate: $6,600 \div 60 = 110$
   Exact: 115 r 34
7. Estimate: $3,500 \div 70 = 50$ Exact: 46 r 30
8. Estimate: $5,400 \div 90 = 60$ Exact: 63
9. Estimate: $4,800 \div 60 = 80$ Exact: 78

Exercise 13, page 72
Estimates will vary.
1. Est.: $360 \div 6 = 60$
   Exact: 58 words per minute
2. Est.: $60 \div 10 = 6$ Exact: 5 years
3. Est.: $\$2,300 \div \$100 = 23$
   Exact: 24 months
4. Est.: $480 \div 40 = 12$ Exact: 13 inches
5. Est.: $360 \div 4 = 90$ Exact: 87 calories

Exercise 14, page 73
Estimates will vary.
1. Estimate: $\$9,600 \div 3 = \$3,200$
   Exact: $3,195
2. Estimate: $\$1,600 \div 80 = \$20$ Exact: $21
3. Estimate: $2,000 - 1,000 = 1,000$
   Exact: 1,017 pounds
4. Estimate: $600 \div 20 = 30$
   Exact: 29 students
5. Est.: $30 \times 10 = 300$ Exact: 336 miles
6. Est.: $\$7,200 \div 12 = \$600$ Exact: $618
7. Est.: $\$650 + \$40 = \$690$ Exact: $686

Division Checkup, page 74
1. 29   3. 19   5. 40 r 3
2. 18   4. 23   6. 32 r 5
7. Est.: $300 \div 6 = 50$ Exact: 52
8. Est.: $280 \div 7 = 40$ Exact: 38
9. Est.: $1,800 \div 60 = 30$ Exact: 27
10. Est.: $600 \div 30 = 20$ Exact: 21 miles
11. Est.: $1,500 \div 30 = 50$ Exact: 48 rows
12. Est.: $720 \div 60 = 12$ Exact: 13 hours

Unit 2: Money

Chapter 8: Money Basics

Exercise 1, page 77
1. 9
2. 3
3. 6
4. 80
5. dimes or tenths
6. tens
7. pennies or hundredths
8. pennies or hundredths
9. ones

Exercise 2, page 78
1. 90¢ or $0.90
2. 6¢ or $0.06
3. $4 or $4.00
4. 30¢ or $0.30
5. $40 or $40.00

Exercise 3, page 79
1. 6¢ or $0.06
2. 60¢ or $0.60
3. $6 or $6.00
4. $100 or $100.00
5. 8¢ or $0.08
6. 5¢ or $0.05
7. c. $0.92
8. b. $5.03

Exercise 4, page 80
1. 5¢ or $0.05
2. 10¢ or $0.10
3. 13¢ or $0.13
4. 80¢ or $0.80
5. 40¢ or $0.40
6. 9¢ or $0.09
7. 54¢ or $0.54
8. 79¢ or $0.79

Exercise 5, page 80
1. $5.20   3. $3.41   5. $40.08
2. $16.09   4. $7.50   6. $12.30

Exercise 6, page 81
1. $6   4. $25   7. $32   10. $209
2. $3   5. $75   8. $20   11. $210
3. $12   6. $90   9. $129   12. $200

Exercise 7, page 82
1. $0.50   5. $2.00   9. $9.00
2. $0.10   6. $1.20   10. $12.60
3. $0.80   7. $4.50   11. $13.00
4. $0.80   8. $5.40   12. $10.00

Exercise 8, page 83
1. $0.19   4. $0.92   7. $3.60
2. $0.45   5. $1.47   8. $2.51
3. $0.09   6. $2.14   9. $6.00

Money Checkup, page 84
1. tens
2. dimes or tenths
3. pennies or hundredths
4. 40¢ or $0.40
5. 6¢ or $0.06
6. $50 or $50.00
7. 4¢ or $0.04
8. 85¢ or $0.85
9. $1.13
10. $20.07
11. $4.30
12. $17.61
13. $8 or $8.00
14. $46.80
15. $3.20

Chapter 9: Calculating with Money

Exercise 1, page 86

1. $234
2. $665
3. $556
4. $201
5. $533
6. $1,192

Exercise 2, page 87

1. $5.17
2. $4.07
3. $11.60
4. $7.03
5. $7.28
6. $9.56

Exercise 3, page 87

1. Est.: $1 + $5 = $6   Exact: $6.39
2. Est.: $4 + $4 = $8   Exact: $7.79
3. Est.: $5 + $6 = $11   Exact: $11.88
4. Est.: $3 + $9 = $12   Exact: $12.35
5. Est.: $2 + $6 = $8   Exact: $8.32
6. Est.: $10 + $8 = $18   Exact: $18.04
7. Est.: $10 + $7 + $7 = $24 Exact: $24.39
8. Est.: $9 + $11 + $29 = $49 Exact: $48.67
9. Est.: $22 + $5 + $11 = $38 Exact: $38.10

Exercise 4, page 88

1. $0.82
2. $7.64
3. $0.32
4. Estimate: $6 − $1 = $5   Exact: $5.10
5. Estimate: $8 − $3 = $5   Exact: $5.49
6. Estimate: $13 − $10 = $3 Exact: $2.51
7. Estimate: $8 − $2 = $6   Exact: $5.44
8. Estimate: $19 − $5 = $14 Exact: $14.09
9. Estimate: $15 − $10 = $5 Exact: $4.27
10. Estimate: $16 − $2 = $14 Exact: $13.55
11. Estimate: $39 − $5 = $34 Exact: $33.64
12. Estimate: $17 − $11 = $6 Exact: $6.29

Exercise 5, page 89

1. $4,896
2. $762
3. $2,340
4. $1,456
5. $1,455
6. $1,196
7. Estimate: $400 × 2 = $800
   Exact: $750
8. Estimate: $9 × 300 = $2,700
   Exact: $2,340
9. Estimate: 7 × $800 = $5,600
   Exact: $5,649
10. Estimate: 500 × $6 = $3,000
    Exact: $3,072
11. Estimate: 8 × $700 = $5,600
    Exact: $5,528
12. Estimate: 400 × $4 = $1,600
    Exact: $1,672

Exercise 6, page 90

1. $1.17
2. $4.06
3. $4.23
4. $4.68
5. $7.20
6. $3.84
7. Estimate: 8 × $6 = $48   Exact: $45.04
8. Estimate: $7 × 4 = $28   Exact: $27.92
9. Estimate: 5 × $7 = $35   Exact: $35.30
10. Estimate: $9 × 7 = $63   Exact: $65.80
11. Estimate: 8 × $6 = $48   Exact: $48.64
12. Estimate: $8 × 6 = $48   Exact: $45.18

Exercise 7, page 91

1. $672
2. $1,675
3. $1,152
4. $27 or $27.00
5. $52.20
6. $28.35
7. Estimate: 28 × 2 = $56
   Exact: $50.12
8. Estimate: $6 × 14 = $84
   Exact: $85.12
9. Estimate: $10 × 25 = $250
   Exact: $245.50
10. Estimate: 31 × $7 = $217
    Exact: $225.06
11. Estimate: 47 × $4 = $188
    Exact: $194.11
12. Estimate: $2 × 53 = $106
    Exact: $99.64

Exercise 8, page 92

1. $4.50
2. $4.25
3. $3.60
4. $11.50
5. $9.75
6. $6.50
7. $9.50
8. $19.20
9. $5.25
10. $16.25
11. $9.40
12. $13.50

Exercise 9, page 93

1. $2.05
2. $4.52
3. $4.15
4. $3.30
5. $7.89
6. $6.28
7. $9.99
8. $2.22
9. $1.68
10. $3.56
11. $8.60
12. $36.18

Exercise 10, page 94

1. $0.082   round down to $0.08
2. $0.135   round up to $0.14
3. $0.128   round up to $0.13
4. $2.265   round up to $2.27
5. $1.723   round down to $1.72
6. $2.535   round up to $2.54
7. $6.348   round up to $6.35
8. $5.936   round up to $5.94

9. $6.362   round down to $6.36
10. $20.677   round up to $20.68
11. $10.704   round down to $10.70
12. $14.147   round up to $14.15

Exercise 11, page 95

1. Est.: $5.60 ÷ 8 = $0.70   Exact: $0.68
2. Est.: $3.00 ÷ 6 = $0.50   Exact: $0.54
3. Est.: $4.00 ÷ 5 = $0.80   Exact: $0.82
4. Est.: $4.20 ÷ 7 = $0.60   Exact: $0.59
5. Est.: $8.10 ÷ 9 = $0.90   Exact: $0.92
6. Est.: $4.00 ÷ 4 = $1.00   Exact: $0.98
7. Est.: $54 ÷ 9 = $6   Exact: $6.28
8. Est.: $35 ÷ 7 = $5   Exact: $4.92
9. Est.: $160 ÷ 8 = $20   Exact: $21.13
10. Est.: $60 ÷ 6 = $10   Exact: $9.79
11. Est.: $32 ÷ 4 = $8   Exact: $8.36
12. Est.: $60 ÷ 5 = $12   Exact: $11.85

Exercise 12, page 96

1. Estimate: $40 + $60 = $100
   Exact: $99.77
2. Estimate: $80 – $73 = $7
   Exact: $7.44
3. Estimate: 8 × $13 = $104
   Exact: $102
4. Estimate: $540 ÷ 90 = $6
   Exact: $6.50
5. Estimate: $3 + $5 + $1 = $9
   Exact: $8.87

Money Checkup, page 97

1. Est.: $13 + $8 = $21   Exact: $20.24
2. Est.: $3 + $15 = $18   Exact: $18.03
3. Est.: $66 – $30 = $36   Exact: $35.84
4. Est.: 8 × $7 = $56   Exact: $58.80
5. Est.: $10 ÷ 5 = $2   Exact: $1.91
6. Est.: $81 ÷ 3 = $27   Exact: $26.92
7. Est.: 38 × $4 = $152   Exact: $155.42
8. Est.: $60 – $50 = $10   Exact: $10.73
9. Est.: $8 × 4 = $32   Exact: $32.48
10. $14.67
11. $5.33
12. Est.: 3 × $18 = $54   Exact: $53.97
13. Est.: $20 – $12 = $8   Exact: $8.40
14. Est. (to nearest 10): $620 + $130 = $750
    Est. (to lead digit): $600 + $100 = $700
    Exact: $746.05
15. Estimate: $480 ÷ 40 = $12
    Exact: $12.35

Unit 3: Decimals

Chapter 10: Decimal Basics

Exercise 1, page 100

1. **a.** 10 equal parts, 5 parts shaded   **b.** 0.5
2. **a.** 10 equal parts, 9 parts shaded   **b.** 0.9
3. **a.** 100 equal parts, 30 parts shaded   **b.** 0.30
4. **a.** 100 equal parts, 60 parts shaded   **b.** 0.60

Exercise 2, page 101

1. 2   5. 2   9. 100
2. 100   6. 7   10. 5
3. thousandths   7. 10
4. 10   8. hundredths

Exercise 3, page 102

1. hundredths   6. thousandths
2. thousandths   7. hundredths
3. tenths   8. tenth
4. hundredths   9. thousandths
5. thousandths   10. thousandths

Exercise 4, page 102

1. 0.06   5. 0.008   9. 0.106
2. 0.004   6. 0.09   10. 0.032
3. 0.012   7. 0.017   11. 0.202
4. 0.096   8. 0.03   12. 0.78

Exercise 5, page 103

1. two and four tenths
2. three and thirty-six hundredths
3. fourteen and two thousandths
4. twenty and nine hundredths
5. fifty and eight tenths
6. nine and thirty-two thousandths
7. five and eleven thousandths
8. sixty-one and seven hundredths

Exercise 6, page 103

1. 80.02   4. 10.21   7. 1.06
2. 4.007   5. 140.5   8. 508.007
3. 19.106   6. 70.903

Answer Key

Exercise 7, page 104

1. 0.57 and 0.570	13. 12.60
2. 0.900 and 0.9	14. 22.20
3. 0.824 and 0.82400	15. 9.00
4. 3.10 and 3.1	16. 25.00
5. 7.45 and 7.450	17. 0.320
6. 5.00 and 5	18. 0.700
7. 20 and 20.00	19. 0.750
8. 36.30 and 36.3	20. 2.180
9. 0.80	21. 7.900
10. 0.50	22. 19.640
11. 1.30	23. 38.000
12. 6.90	24. 50.000

Exercise 8, page 105

1. 0.36 or .36	4. 3	7. 28
2. 0.7 or .7	5. 5.6	8. 2.505
3. 0.04 or .04	6. 10.01	9. 14.1

Exercise 9, page 106

1. 0.4	5. 0.08	9. 0.1	13. 0.443
2. 0.9	6. 0.29	10. 0.81	14. 0.115
3. 0.17	7. 0.7	11. 0.07	15. 0.37
4. 0.572	8. 0.528	12. 0.9	

Exercise 10, page 107

1. 15	4. 0.5	7. 0.04
2. 126	5. 62.9	8. 6.26
3. 10	6. 6.4	9. 56.91

Decimal Checkup, page 108

1. tenths	9. 0.4 or .4
2. hundredths	10. 9.07
3. thousandths	11. 17.008
4. 10	12. 0.250
5. 100	13. 0.38 and 0.380
6. thousandths	14. 0.41
7. 0.11 or .11	15. 0.5
8. 0.053 or .053	16. 18.21

Chapter 11: Calculating with Decimals

Exercise 1, page 110

1. 0.67	5. 0.9	9. 28.69
2. 0.549	6. 16.276	10. 2.853
3. 11.794	7. 25.762	11. 17.99
4. 4.759	8. 0.968	12. 6.713

Exercise 2, page 111

1. 0.54	5. 2.84	9. 4.447
2. 0.291	6. 2.55	10. 0.335
3. 0.156	7. 7.402	11. 1.63
4. 3.125	8. 5.17	12. 23.8

Exercise 3, page 112

1. 76	5. 2.412	9. 0.344
2. 2.76	6. 12.48	10. 0.945
3. 2.34	7. 1.252	11. 0.9
4. 0.203	8. 0.194	12. 1.41

Exercise 4, page 113

1. 6.30 = 6.3	5. 42.150 = 42.15
2. 18.3	6. 87.2
3. 3.25	7. 77.4
4. 18.96	8. 11.60 = 11.6

Exercise 5, page 113

1. 4.5	6. 3.87
2. 5.6	7. 1.40 = 1.4
3. 2.08	8. 2.032
4. 0.535	
5. 1.05	

Exercise 6, page 114

1. 2.508	6. 2.286
2. 17.98	7. 7.294
3. 2.175	8. 32.40 = 32.4
4. 97.72	9. 5.292
5. 139.36	

Exercise 7, page 115

1. 26	4. 7.7	7. 4.4	10. 88
2. 1.29	5. 860	8. 709	11. 650
3. 40.3	6. 5,120	9. 4,600	12. 2

Exercise 8, page 116

1. 0.55	7. 0.65
2. 0.13	8. 0.06
3. 1.7	9. 0.36
4. 2.316... ≈ 2.32	10. 0.514 ≈ 0.51
5. 0.38	11. 2.51
6. 2.255... ≈ 2.26	12. 0.328... ≈ 0.33

Exercise 9, page 117

1. $12. \overline{)276.}$
2. $3. \overline{)37.5}$
3. $8. \overline{)5,920.}$
4. $7. \overline{)2.52}$
5. $16. \overline{)72.}$
6. $32. \overline{)7,680.}$

Exercise 10, page 118

1. 27
2. 120
3. 0.25
4. 3.21
5. $33.333\ldots \approx 33.33$
6. 500
7. 17.5
8. $0.355\ldots \approx 0.36$
9. 40
10. 12
11. 2.4
12. $8.666\ldots \approx 8.67$

Exercise 11, page 119

1. 0.52
2. 4.7
3. 1.25
4. $4.20
5. 0.293
6. 0.087
7. 0.006
8. $0.23 or 23¢
9. 0.405
10. 0.071
11. 8.569
12. $0.06 or 6¢

Exercise 12, pages 120–121

1. Est.: $4 - 3 = 1$ Exact: 0.76 pound
2. Est.: $2 \times 3 = 6$ Exact: 6.25 ounces
3. Est.: $24 \div 6 = 4$
   Exact: 4.05 fluid ounces
4. Est.: $2 + 2 = 4$ Exact: 3.79 pounds
5. Est.: $315 \div 5 = 63$
   Exact: $62.98 \approx 63.0$ miles
6. Est.: $100 \times 1 = 100$ Exact: 132 pounds
7. Est.: $2 \times 65 = 130$ Exact: 104 miles
8. Est.: $99 + 6 = 105$ Exact: 104.4 degrees
9. Est.: $6 + 2 = 8$ Exact: 7.45 inches
10. Est.: $150 \div 3 = 50$ Exact: 61.2 miles

Decimal Checkup, page 122

1. 29.613
2. 1.488
3. 3.613
4. 11.75
5. 43.75
6. 2.608
7. 7.38
8. 409
9. 0.36
10. 2.05
11. 0.367
12. 0.050 or 0.05
13. Est.: $400 \times 2 = 800$ Exact: 819 miles
14. Est.: $4 - 1 = 3$ Exact: 2.25 meters
15. Est.: $7 + 4 + 2 = 13$ Exact: 13.15 pounds
16. Est.: $75 \div 5 = 15 Exact: $16.76

Unit 4: Fractions

Chapter 12: Fractions Basics

Exercise 1, page 125

1. 4
2. $\frac{1}{4}$
3. 5
4. $\frac{1}{5}$
5. 8
6. $\frac{1}{8}$

Exercise 2, page 126

1. a. $\frac{8}{8}$ b. $\frac{3}{8}$ c. $\frac{5}{8}$
2. a. $\frac{3}{3}$ b. $\frac{2}{3}$ c. $\frac{1}{3}$
3. a. $\frac{5}{5}$ b. $\frac{3}{5}$ c. $\frac{2}{5}$
4. a. $\frac{12}{12}$ b. $\frac{8}{12}$ c. $\frac{4}{12}$

Exercise 3, page 127

1. $\frac{1}{3}$ (Thirds are larger parts than fourths.)
2. $\frac{1}{2}$ (Halves are larger parts than fourths.)
3. $\frac{1}{3}$ (Thirds are larger parts than eighths.)
4. $\frac{1}{2}$ (Halves are larger parts than fifths.)
5. $\frac{1}{8}$ (Eighths are larger parts than tenths.)
6. $\frac{1}{3}$ (Thirds are larger parts than ninths.)
7. $\frac{1}{6}$ (Sixths are larger parts than twelfths.)
8. $\frac{1}{9}$ (Ninths are larger parts than twelfths.)
9. $\frac{1}{10}$ (Tenths are larger parts than twentieths.)

Exercise 4, page 128

1. $\frac{3}{4}$
2. $\frac{2}{3}$
3. $\frac{3}{5}$
4. $\frac{3}{4}$
5. $\frac{1}{2}$
6. $\frac{7}{12}$

Exercise 5, page 129

1. $\frac{20}{10}$
2. $\frac{16}{16}$
3. $\frac{4}{2}$

Exercise 6, page 129

1. $\frac{7}{4}$
2. $\frac{24}{16}$
3. $\frac{14}{6}$

Exercise 7, page 130

1. a. $1\frac{1}{4}$ b. $2\frac{3}{4}$ c. $3\frac{2}{4}$ or $3\frac{1}{2}$

2. a. $1\frac{4}{16}$ or $1\frac{1}{4}$ b. $2\frac{8}{16}$ or $2\frac{1}{2}$
   c. $2\frac{15}{16}$ d. $3\frac{10}{16}$ or $3\frac{5}{8}$

3. $1\frac{1}{3}$ 5. $3\frac{5}{16}$ 7. $6\frac{1}{2}$

4. $4\frac{3}{4}$ 6. $3\frac{7}{12}$

Exercise 8, page 131

1. $\frac{8}{16}$ 3. $\frac{9}{18}$ 5. $\frac{12}{24}$
2. more   4. less   6. more
                      7. less

Exercise 9, page 132

1. 1   4. 2   7. 6   10. 16
2. 3   5. 4   8. 7   11. 20
3. 3   6. 6   9. 11   12. 25

Fraction Checkup, page 133

1. $\frac{5}{8}$ 5. $\frac{14}{28}$ 10. $6\frac{1}{2}$
2. $\frac{2}{3}$ 6. $\frac{1}{4}$ 11. $2\frac{3}{4}$
3. $\frac{5}{6}$ 7. $\frac{2}{5}$ 12. 7
4. a. $\frac{1}{8}$ 8. $\frac{1}{3}$ 13. 10
   b. $\frac{6}{8}$ or $\frac{3}{4}$ 9. $\frac{3}{8}$ 14. 9
   c. $1\frac{4}{8}$ or $1\frac{1}{2}$

Chapter 13: Equivalent Fractions

Exercise 1, page 135

1. $\frac{3}{6}$ 3. $\frac{6}{8}$ 5. $\frac{6}{15}$ 7. $\frac{9}{24}$
2. $\frac{2}{6}$ 4. $\frac{4}{10}$ 6. $\frac{10}{12}$ 8. $\frac{6}{9}$

Exercise 2, page 136

1. $\frac{2}{4}$ and $\frac{1}{4}$ 6. $\frac{3}{10}$ and $\frac{8}{10}$
2. $\frac{2}{6}$ and $\frac{1}{6}$ 7. $\frac{20}{36}, \frac{6}{36},$ and $\frac{21}{36}$
3. $\frac{3}{12}$ and $\frac{8}{12}$ 8. $\frac{7}{28}, \frac{12}{28},$ and $\frac{14}{28}$
4. $\frac{6}{15}$ and $\frac{5}{15}$ 9. $\frac{8}{30}, \frac{18}{30},$ and $\frac{25}{30}$
5. $\frac{15}{20}$ and $\frac{8}{20}$

Exercise 3, page 137

1. $\frac{1}{2}$ 4. $\frac{1}{3}$ 7. $\frac{3}{4}$ 10. $\frac{5}{9}$
2. $\frac{3}{8}$ 5. $\frac{2}{3}$ 8. $\frac{2}{3}$
3. $\frac{1}{2}$ 6. $\frac{3}{5}$ 9. $\frac{1}{3}$

Exercise 4, page 138

1. $\frac{8}{10} = \frac{4}{5}$ 4. $\frac{75}{100} = \frac{3}{4}$
2. $\frac{25}{100} = \frac{1}{4}$ 5. $\frac{4}{100} = \frac{1}{25}$
3. $\frac{6}{10} = \frac{3}{5}$

Exercise 5, page 138

1. 0.25   3. 0.833   5. 0.35
2. 0.125   4. 0.6

Exercise 6, page 139

1. $1\frac{1}{2} = \frac{3}{2}$ 2. $1\frac{6}{8} = \frac{14}{8}$ 3. $2\frac{2}{3} = \frac{8}{3}$

Exercise 7, page 139

1. $\frac{17}{4}$ 5. $\frac{7}{2}$ 9. $\frac{17}{6}$

2. $\frac{5}{2}$ 6. $\frac{22}{5}$ 10. $\frac{19}{12}$

3. $\frac{5}{3}$ 7. $\frac{7}{3}$

4. $\frac{7}{4}$ 8. $\frac{31}{8}$

Exercise 8, page 140

1. 2   3. $3\frac{1}{3}$ 5. $1\frac{5}{8}$

2. 1   4. $4\frac{1}{6}$

Exercise 9, page 140

1. 2.25   3. 2.4   5. 4.167

2. 3.5   4. 1.75

Fractions Checkup, page 141

1. $\frac{3}{4} = \frac{6}{8} = \frac{9}{12} = \frac{12}{16} = \frac{15}{20}$

2. $\frac{2}{3} = \frac{4}{6} = \frac{6}{9} = \frac{8}{12} = \frac{10}{15}$

3. $\frac{4}{5} = \frac{8}{10} = \frac{12}{15} = \frac{16}{20} = \frac{20}{25}$

4. $\frac{9}{15}$ and $\frac{5}{15}$ 5. $\frac{4}{8}$ and $\frac{7}{8}$

6. $\frac{18}{24}, \frac{20}{24}$, and $\frac{9}{24}$

7. $\frac{1}{2}$ 10. $\frac{5}{2}$ 13. $3\frac{3}{4}$ 16. 0.4

8. $\frac{1}{4}$ 11. $\frac{15}{4}$ 14. $1\frac{4}{5}$ 17. 1.375

9. $\frac{7}{8}$ 12. $\frac{21}{5}$ 15. $4\frac{2}{3}$ 18. 5.5

Chapter 14: Calculating with Fractions

Exercise 1, page 143

1. $\frac{4}{5}$ 3. $\frac{13}{16}$

2. $\frac{6}{4} = 1\frac{2}{4} = 1\frac{1}{2}$ 4. $\frac{3}{2} = 1\frac{1}{2}$

Exercise 2, page 144

1. $\frac{5}{4} = 1\frac{1}{4}$ 7. $\frac{13}{12} = 1\frac{1}{12}$

2. $\frac{5}{6}$ 8. $\frac{11}{8} = 1\frac{3}{8}$

3. $\frac{13}{10} = 1\frac{3}{10}$ 9. $\frac{17}{16} = 1\frac{1}{16}$

4. $\frac{5}{8}$ 10. $\frac{13}{8} = 1\frac{5}{8}$

5. $\frac{13}{10} = 1\frac{3}{10}$ 11. $\frac{18}{12} = 1\frac{6}{12} = 1\frac{1}{2}$

6. $\frac{11}{12}$ 12. $\frac{13}{12} = 1\frac{1}{12}$

Exercise 3, page 145

1. Estimate: $2 + 3 = 5$ Exact: $5\frac{2}{4} = 5\frac{1}{2}$

2. Estimate: $4 + 2 = 6$ Exact: $6\frac{4}{8} = 6\frac{1}{2}$

3. Estimate: $2 + 4 = 6$ Exact: $4\frac{12}{10} = 5\frac{1}{5}$

4. Estimate: $2 + 4 = 6$ Exact: $4\frac{11}{8} = 5\frac{3}{8}$

5. Estimate: $3 + 3 = 6$ Exact: $4\frac{7}{6} = 5\frac{1}{6}$

6. Estimate: $5 + 3 = 8$ Exact: $7\frac{4}{4} = 8$

7. Estimate: $4 + 3 = 7$ Exact: $6\frac{8}{8} = 7$

8. Estimate: $6 + 3 = 9$ Exact: $7\frac{8}{6} = 8\frac{1}{3}$

9. Estimate: $4 + 5 = 9$ Exact: $7\frac{13}{8} = 8\frac{5}{8}$

10. Estimate: $2 + 5 = 7$ Exact: $5\frac{9}{8} = 6\frac{1}{8}$

11. Estimate: $7 + 5 = 12$ Exact: $10\frac{19}{12} = 11\frac{7}{12}$

12. Estimate: $3 + 6 = 9$ Exact: $7\frac{7}{6} = 8\frac{1}{6}$

Answer Key

Exercise 4, page 146

1. $\frac{1}{3}$ 3. $\frac{7}{12}$

2. $\frac{3}{8}$ 4. $\frac{4}{10} = \frac{2}{5}$

Exercise 5, page 146

1. $\frac{1}{4}$ 4. $\frac{1}{6}$ 7. $\frac{9}{16}$

2. $\frac{1}{6}$ 5. $\frac{3}{8}$ 8. $\frac{1}{12}$

3. $\frac{5}{10} = \frac{1}{2}$ 6. $\frac{7}{15}$

Exercise 6, page 147

1. $\frac{3}{3}$ 3. $\frac{5}{5}$ 5. $\frac{8}{8}$ 7. $\frac{4}{4}$

2. $\frac{2}{2}$ 4. $\frac{10}{10}$ 6. $\frac{16}{16}$ 8. $\frac{6}{6}$

Exercise 7, page 147

1. $\frac{1}{3}$ 4. $2\frac{1}{5}$ 7. $8\frac{1}{2}$

2. $\frac{1}{4}$ 5. $4\frac{1}{4}$ 8. $6\frac{1}{3}$

3. $1\frac{5}{8}$ 6. $2\frac{1}{10}$ 9. $7\frac{1}{2}$

Exercise 8, page 148

1. Estimate: $3 - 1 = 2$ Exact: $1\frac{1}{3}$

2. Estimate: $5 - 2 = 3$ Exact: $2\frac{2}{4} = 2\frac{1}{2}$

3. Estimate: $3 - 2 = 1$ Exact: $1\frac{1}{5}$

4. Estimate: $6 - 1 = 5$ Exact: $4\frac{1}{4}$

5. Estimate: $5 - 1 = 4$ Exact: $3\frac{1}{8}$

6. Estimate: $6 - 2 = 4$ Exact: $3\frac{1}{6}$

7. Estimate: $8 - 4 = 4$ Exact: $4\frac{2}{4} = 4\frac{1}{2}$

8. Estimate: $7 - 5 = 2$ Exact: $2\frac{3}{5}$

9. Estimate: $7 - 4 = 3$ Exact: $2\frac{5}{6}$

10. Estimate: $4 - 3 = 1$ Exact: $1\frac{1}{2}$

11. Estimate: $8 - 6 = 2$ Exact: $2\frac{1}{8}$

12. Estimate: $9 - 8 = 1$ Exact: $1\frac{3}{4}$

Exercise 9, page 149

1. $\frac{1}{2} \times \frac{3}{4} = \frac{3}{8}$ yard

2. $\frac{1}{4} \times \frac{1}{2} = \frac{1}{8}$ gallon

3. $\frac{1}{3} \times \frac{9}{10} = \frac{9}{30} = \frac{3}{10}$ mile

4. $\frac{1}{2} \times \frac{1}{2} = \frac{1}{4}$ dollar

5. $\frac{1}{4} \times \frac{1}{4} = \frac{1}{16}$ pound

6. $\frac{1}{3} \times \frac{3}{4} = \frac{3}{12} = \frac{1}{4}$ hour

7. $\frac{6}{12} = \frac{1}{2}$

8. $\frac{15}{48} = \frac{5}{16}$

9. $\frac{3}{60} = \frac{1}{20}$

10. $\frac{12}{20} = \frac{3}{5}$

11. $\frac{10}{24} = \frac{5}{12}$

12. $\frac{35}{60} = \frac{7}{12}$

Exercise 10, page 150

1. $\frac{3}{16}$ 5. $\frac{3}{4}$ 9. $\frac{2}{15}$

2. $\frac{14}{27}$ 6. $\frac{3}{20}$ 10. $\frac{4}{9}$

3. $\frac{3}{5}$ 7. $\frac{1}{4}$ 11. $\frac{9}{16}$

4. $\frac{3}{10}$ 8. $\frac{3}{4}$ 12. $\frac{3}{10}$

Exercise 11, page 151

1. 6   5. $1\frac{1}{4}$ 9. $5\frac{1}{4}$

2. 8   6. 6   10. 10

3. $6\frac{3}{4}$ 7. $9\frac{3}{5}$ 11. $4\frac{1}{2}$

4. $7\frac{1}{2}$ 8. $2\frac{2}{5}$ 12. 4

Exercise 12, page 152

1. Estimate: $\frac{1}{2} \times 2 = 1$ Exact: $\frac{3}{4}$

2. Estimate: $\frac{1}{3} \times 4 = 1\frac{1}{3}$ Exact: $1\frac{1}{6}$

3. Estimate: $\frac{1}{4} \times 5 = 1\frac{1}{4}$ Exact: $1\frac{3}{16}$

4. Estimate: $\frac{3}{4} \times 6 = 4\frac{1}{2}$ Exact: $4\frac{1}{8}$

5. Estimate: $\frac{2}{3} \times 6 = 4$ Exact: $4\frac{2}{9}$

6. Estimate: $\frac{1}{2} \times 7 = 3\frac{1}{2}$ Exact: $3\frac{5}{8}$

7. Estimate: $\frac{1}{3} \times 5 = 1\frac{2}{3}$ Exact: $1\frac{3}{4}$

8. Estimate: $\frac{1}{2} \times 7 = 3\frac{1}{2}$ Exact: $3\frac{3}{8}$

Exercise 13, page 153

1. $\frac{2}{1}$ 3. $\frac{8}{5}$ 5. $\frac{16}{7}$

2. $\frac{4}{3}$ 4. $\frac{10}{3}$

Exercise 14, page 153

1. 12   3. $5\frac{3}{5}$ 5. $2\frac{7}{10}$ 7. $6\frac{1}{4}$

2. 14   4. 9   6. 25   8. $9\frac{1}{3}$

Exercise 15, page 154

1. $3\frac{1}{2} = \frac{7}{2}$ $\frac{2}{7}$ 4. $8 = \frac{8}{1}$ $\frac{1}{8}$

2. $4\frac{2}{3} = \frac{14}{3}$ $\frac{3}{14}$

3. $1\frac{5}{8} = \frac{13}{8}$ $\frac{8}{13}$

Exercise 16, page 154

1. Estimate: $3 \div 2 = 1\frac{1}{2}$ Exact: $1\frac{1}{4}$

2. Estimate: $2 \div 4 = \frac{1}{2}$ Exact: $\frac{7}{16}$

3. Estimate: $5 \div 1 = 5$ Exact: $3\frac{1}{2}$

4. Estimate: $7 \div 2 = 3\frac{1}{2}$ Exact: $4\frac{1}{3}$

5. Estimate: $1 \div 3 = \frac{1}{3}$ Exact: $\frac{1}{4}$

6. Estimate: $1 \div 5 = \frac{1}{5}$ Exact: $\frac{1}{10}$

7. Estimate: $9 \div 1 = 9$ Exact: 7

8. Estimate: $1 \div 1 = 1$ Exact: $\frac{1}{2}$

Exercise 17, page 155

1. Est.: $3 \times \$12 = \$36$ Exact: $33

2. Est.: $2 + 5 = 7$ Exact: $6\frac{1}{4}$ miles

3. Est.: $6 - 4 = 2$ Exact: $1\frac{2}{3}$ gallons

4. Est.: $4 \times 64 = 256$ Exact: 224 miles

5. Est.: $9 \div 2 = 4\frac{1}{2}$ Exact: 6 shelves

6. Est.: $70 + 4 = 74$ Exact: 73 inches

Answer Key

Fractions Checkup, page 156

1. $\frac{3}{4}$
2. $1\frac{4}{15}$
3. $4\frac{1}{4}$
4. $\frac{3}{4}$
5. $\frac{1}{8}$
6. $3\frac{2}{3}$
7. $\frac{3}{8}$
8. 2
9. 10
10. $\frac{9}{10}$
11. 10
12. $1\frac{5}{8}$

13. Est.: $30 - 16 = 14$ Exact: $14\frac{1}{4}$ inches
14. Est.: $3 + 1 = 4$ Exact: $\$3\frac{4}{5}$ million
15. Est.: $3 \times \$8 = \$24$ Exact: $26.25
16. Est.: $20 \div 3 = 6\frac{2}{3}$ Exact: 8 books

Unit 5: Ratio and Percent

Chapter 15: Ratio Basics

Exercise 1, page 159

1. 9 to 11
2. 4 to 7
3. 7 : 12
4. 5 : 28
5. $\frac{63}{80}$
6. $\frac{11}{16}$

Exercise 2, page 160

1. 1 to 2
2. 3 : 2
3. 3 to 1
4. 2 : 1
5. 3 : 5
6. 1 to 2
7. 3 : 4
8. 6 to 5

Exercise 3, page 160

1. $3 : 24 = 1 : 8$
2. $15 : 25 = 3 : 5$
3. $288 : 12 = 24 : 1$

Exercise 4, page 161

1. 23 miles per hour
2. 6 tables per server
3. 27 students per classroom
4. 26 miles per gallon
5. $42 per month
6. 36 seats per row
7. 72 heartbeats per minute
8. 3.2 children per family

Exercise 5, page 162

1. a. $12 : 20 = 3 : 5$
   b. $12 : 8 = 3 : 2$
   c. $8 : 20 = 2 : 5$
2. a. $108 : 54 = 2 : 1$
   b. $108 : 162 = 2 : 3$
   c. $54 : 162 = 1 : 3$
3. a. $9 : 36 = 1 : 4$
   b. $9 : 45 = 1 : 5$
   c. $36 : 45 = 4 : 5$

Exercise 6, page 163

Cross products can be in any order.

1. a. $2 \times 12 = 24$
   b. $3 \times 8 = 24$
2. a. $3 \times 16 = 48$
   b. $4 \times 12 = 48$
3. a. $1 \times 30 = 30$
   b. $6 \times 5 = 30$
4. a. $7 \times 40 = 280$
   b. $10 \times 28 = 280$
5. a. $5 \times 8 = 40$
   b. $20 \times 2 = 40$
6. a. $16 \times 3 = 48$
   b. $24 \times 2 = 48$
7. a. $9 \times 16 = 144$
   b. $12 \times 12 = 144$
8. a. $5 \times 18 = 90$
   b. $10 \times 9 = 90$

Exercise 7, page 164

1. $u = 9$ $3 \times 15 = 45; 5 \times 9 = 45$
2. $x = 1$ $1 \times 27 = 27; 9 \times 3 = 27$
3. $g = 2$ $2 \times 15 = 30; 6 \times 5 = 30$
4. $a = 5$ $4 \times 20 = 80; 5 \times 16 = 80$
5. $r = 3$ $1.5 \times 6 = 9; 3 \times 3 = 9$
6. $x = 10$ $5 \times 18 = 90; 9 \times 10 = 90$
7. $e = 20$ $7 \times 100 = 700; 20 \times 35 = 700$
8. $n = 9$ $4 \times 180 = 720; 9 \times 80 = 720$

Exercise 8, page 165

1. 100 men
2. 18 inches
3. 312 miles
4. $56.25
5. 290 miles
6. 162 households

Exercise 9, page 166

1. a. 9 : 1
   b. 1 : 10
   c. 9 : 10
   d. 200 problems
2. a. 5 : 3
   b. 3 : 8
   c. 5 : 8
   d. 60 women

Ratio Checkup, page 167

1. $9 : 12 = 3 : 4$
2. $16 : 20 = 4 : 5$
3. $50 : 2 = 25 : 1$
4. 45 words per minute
5. 23 miles per gallon
6. 32 students per class
7. a. $120 : 30 = 4 : 1$
   b. $120 : 150 = 4 : 5$
   c. $30 : 150 = 1 : 5$
8. $x = 96$
9. $c = 40$
10. $m = 5$
11. $3\frac{1}{3}$ inches
12. 60 people

Chapter 16: Percent Basics

Exercise 1, page 169

1. a. $\frac{7}{10} = \frac{70}{100}$ 70 percent is shaded.

   b. $\frac{3}{10} = \frac{30}{100}$ 30 percent is unshaded.

2. a. $\frac{2}{10} = \frac{20}{100}$ 20 percent is shaded.

   b. $\frac{8}{10} = \frac{80}{100}$ 80 percent is unshaded.

3. 25 percent = 25%
4. 15 percent = 15%
5. 7 percent = 7%
6. 18 percent = 18%
7. forty-two percent = 42%

Exercise 2, page 170

1. a. 60 questions
   b. 15 math questions
   c. 45 reading questions
2. a. $60 winnings
   b. $9 tax
   c. $51 net cash
3. a. 20 coins
   b. 4 dimes
   c. 6 pennies
   d. 10 nickels

4. a. 200 invitations
   b. 96 yes
   c. 44 no
   d. 60 no reply

Exercise 3, page 171

1. $0.10 = 0.1$
2. 0.05
3. 0.42
4. 0.25
5. 0.75
6. $0.80 = 0.8$
7. 0.045
8. $3.00 = 3$
9. $1.20 = 1.2$

Exercise 4, page 171

1. $\frac{10}{100} = \frac{1}{10}$
2. $\frac{5}{100} = \frac{1}{20}$
3. $\frac{42}{100} = \frac{21}{50}$
4. $\frac{25}{100} = \frac{1}{4}$
5. $\frac{75}{100} = \frac{3}{4}$
6. $\frac{80}{100} = \frac{4}{5}$
7. $\frac{30}{100} = \frac{3}{10}$
8. $\frac{95}{100} = \frac{19}{20}$
9. $\frac{125}{100} = \frac{5}{4}$ or $1\frac{1}{4}$

Exercise 5, page 172

1. $0.25 \times 80 = 20$
2. $0.08 \times 240 = 19.2$
3. $0.5 \times 92 = 46$
4. $0.3 \times 200 = 60$
5. $0.45 \times 120 = 54$
6. $0.75 \times 64 = 48$
7. $0.9 \times 450 = 405$
8. $0.015 \times 300 = 4.5$
9. $1.5 \times 60 = 90$
10. $0.25 \times 20 = 5$
11. $0.15 \times 20 = 3$
12. $0.2 \times 20 = 4$
13. $0.3 \times 20 = 6$
14. $0.1 \times 20 = 2$

Exercise 6, page 173

1. $\frac{1}{4} \times 60 = 15$
2. $\frac{2}{5} \times 140 = 56$
3. $\frac{1}{10} \times 250 = 25$
4. $\frac{1}{2} \times 82 = 41$
5. $\frac{7}{20} \times 120 = 42$
6. $\frac{3}{4} \times 144 = 108$
7. $\frac{4}{5} \times 250 = 200$
8. $\frac{9}{10} \times 70 = 63$
9. $\frac{3}{2} \times 18 = 27$
10. $\frac{1}{4} \times 20 = 5$
11. $\frac{3}{20} \times 20 = 3$
12. $\frac{1}{5} \times 20 = 4$
13. $\frac{3}{10} \times 20 = 6$
14. $\frac{1}{10} \times 20 = 2$

Answer Key

Exercise 7, page 174

1. $0.4 \times 45 = 18$
2. $\frac{1}{3} \times 75 = 25$
3. $\frac{5}{8} \times 72 = 45$
4. $\frac{3}{4} \times 80 = 60$
5. $\frac{1}{6} \times 120 = 20$
6. $0.6 \times 150 = 90$
7. $\frac{2}{3} \times 300 = 200$
8. $\frac{3}{8} \times 400 = 150$
9. $\frac{1}{2} \times 240 = 120$

Exercise 8, page 175

1. **a.** $0.7 \times 120 = 84$ questions
   b. $\frac{7}{10} \times 120 = 84$ questions
2. **a.** $0.15 \times \$28 = \$4.20$
   b. $\frac{3}{20} \times \$28 = \$4\frac{1}{5} = \$4.20$
3. **a.** $0.8 \times \$85 = \$68$
   b. $\frac{4}{5} \times \$85 = \$68$
4. **a.** $0.1 \times \$2,500 = \$250$
   b. $\frac{1}{10} \times \$2,500 = \$250$
5. **a.** $0.3 \times 2,800 = 840$ calories
   b. $\frac{3}{10} \times 2,800 = 840$ calories

Exercise 9, page 176

1. $501.50
2. $646.60
3. $21.16
4. 176.4 pounds
5. $188,500
6. $94.34
7. $2,800
8. $2,240

Exercise 10, page 177

1. $\frac{15}{30} = \frac{1}{2} = 50\%$
2. $\frac{24}{240} = \frac{1}{10} = 10\%$
3. $\frac{18}{54} = \frac{1}{3} = 33\frac{1}{3}\%$
4. $\frac{28}{35} = \frac{4}{5} = 80\%$
5. $\frac{12}{72} = \frac{1}{6} = 16\frac{2}{3}\%$
6. $\frac{8}{200} = \frac{4}{100} = 4\%$
7. $\frac{16}{64} = \frac{1}{4} = 25\%$
8. $\frac{45}{75} = \frac{3}{5} = 60\%$
9. $\frac{60}{80} = \frac{3}{4} = 75\%$
10. $\frac{90}{720} = \frac{1}{8} = 12\frac{1}{2}\%$
11. $\frac{18}{20} = \frac{9}{10} = 90\%$
12. $\frac{700}{2,800} = \frac{1}{4} = 25\%$
13. $\frac{12}{30} = \frac{2}{5} = 40\%$

Percent Checkup, page 178

1. **a.** $0.60 = 0.6$
   b. 0.12
   c. 0.03
2. **a.** $3/20$
   b. $40/100 = 2/5$
   c. $4/100 = 1/25$
3. $2,400
4. $0.3 \times \$2,400 = \$720$
5. $0.2 \times \$2,400 = \$480$
6. $\frac{1}{4} \times \$2,400 = \$600$
7. $0.05 \times \$2,400 = \$120$
8. $0.35 \times 400 = 140$
9. $\frac{1}{3} \times 810 = 270$
10. $\frac{18}{24} = \frac{3}{4}; \frac{3}{4} \times 100\% = 75\%$